Alex Kerr

Author of *Lost Japan* and *D...*

T0082303

Hidden Japan

An Astonishing World of Thatched Villages,
Ancient Shrines and Primeval Forests

TUTTLE Publishing

Tokyo │ Rutland, Vermont │ Singapore

"Books to Span the East and West"

Tuttle Publishing was founded in 1832 in the small New England town of Rutland, Vermont [USA]. Our core values remain as strong today as they were then—to publish best-in-class books which bring people together one page at a time. In 1948, we established a publishing outpost in Japan—and Tuttle is now a leader in publishing English-language books about the arts, languages and cultures of Asia. The world has become a much smaller place today and Asia's economic and cultural influence has grown. Yet the need for meaningful dialogue and information about this diverse region has never been greater. Over the past seven decades, Tuttle has published thousands of books on subjects ranging from martial arts and paper crafts to language learning and literature—and our talented authors, illustrators, designers and photographers have won many prestigious awards. We welcome you to explore the wealth of information available on Asia at www.tuttlepublishing.com.

Published by Tuttle Publishing, an imprint of Periplus Editions (HK) Ltd.

www.tuttlepublishing.com

Copyright ©2023 Periplus Editions (HK) Ltd

Unless otherwise noted, all photographs are by Alex Kerr and Ohshima Atsuyuki.

ISBN: 978-4-8053-1751-8

27 26 25 24 23
10 9 8 7 6 5 4 3 2 1   2304TP

Printed in Singapore

TUTTLE PUBLISHING® is a registered trademark of Tuttle Publishing, a division of Periplus Editions (HK) Ltd.

Distributed by

North America,
Latin America & Europe
Tuttle Publishing
364 Innovation Drive
North Clarendon, VT 05759-9436 U.S.A.
Tel: 1 (802) 773-8930
Fax: 1 (802) 773-6993
info@tuttlepublishing.com
www.tuttlepublishing.com

Japan
Tuttle Publishing
Yaekari Building
3rd Floor, 5-4-12 Osaki
Shinagawa-ku, Tokyo 141 0032
Tel: (81) 3 5437-0171
Fax: (81) 3 5437-0755
sales@tuttle.co.jp
www.tuttle.co.jp

Asia Pacific
Berkeley Books Pte Ltd
3 Kallang Sector #04-01
Singapore 349278
Tel: (65) 6741 2178
Fax: (65) 6741 2179
inquiries@periplus.com.sg
www.tuttlepublishing.com

Contents

Map of Japan

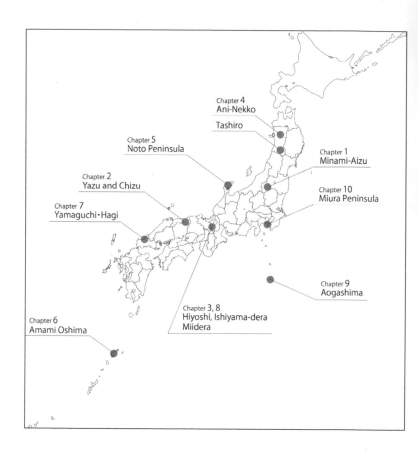

Introduction
Japan's Hidden Places

This book describes visits I made from 2017 to 2019 to ten "hidden places" in Japan. These included not only remote hamlets in Akita and Tottori prefectures, but some easily accessible places that have nevertheless been overlooked and forgotten. I was seeking the Japan I have loved since I was a child.

In my book *Dogs and Demons* (2001) I predicted that as Japan's countryside continued to be ravaged by poorly planned public works and littered with concrete and garish signage, this would have a detrimental effect on foreign travelers, who would be repelled by the ugliness they saw. I was completely wrong. Foreign visitors have mostly overlooked it all. It's because visitors to Japan come in search of beauty, and naturally enough focus on the beautiful. And they have no way of knowing how drastic the changes have been.

That's not the case with the Japanese. There are many who feel the same sorrow at what has overtaken their country as I do. They're seeking the beautiful Japan which is increasingly hard to find, but which they know must still be there. This book was written for them and was originally published in Japanese in December 2020 under the title *Nippon junrei* [Japan pilgrimage]. After it came out, a number of foreign friends asked me if it could be translated into English. This book is that translation, but while I aimed to stay close to the original, I ended up making additions here and there. Sometimes it was to clarify the meaning for people who don't live in Japan, and other times because the work of translation sparked new thoughts. A few of these changes are significant expansions on the Japanese book—and now I wish I could go back and rewrite it to include them.

Even with these revisions, my way of approaching things in this book is not how I would normally have written in English, and at times the rhyme and rhythm of things may sound a bit odd to foreign readers. More unsettling than this, however, will likely be the sense of the fragility of the landscapes I describe.

This is not a full description of the places I visited. That's the role of guidebooks. Instead, I focus on one or two particular points that draw my interest—the line of a temple roof, the shape of a rice paddy or a mountainside covered with primeval trees. It's such details that take us to a deeper place.

Even many Japanese would no longer be aware, for example, that the shape of rice paddies has changed in recent decades. Once you know that, you start to look at rice paddies differently. This book is an exploration of not only forgotten places, but forgotten details.

A few years ago, I read an account by a foreign writer in which he walked the Kumano Pilgrimage, a series of ancient trails through the forests of the Kii Peninsula, imagining how this scenery must have pleased the great print artist Hiroshige. No matter that Hiroshige never came near the site of this pilgrimage. More critically, the industrial cedar plantations that now cover the Kumano route look nothing like the forests of the Edo period.

Suppose we wanted to ask ourselves what really is wonderful about the Kumano Pilgrimage. If the romance does not lie in Hiroshige or in cedar plantations, then where and what is it?

In *Hidden Japan*, I try to return to where the romance is really to be found. Secluded hamlets like something out of an old ink painting do still exist, as do temples and shrines in remote areas that survived the wars that wiped out old Kyoto and Edo and the tourist frenzy of recent years. Haunted woods old enough to have enchanted Hiroshige and Basho still stand. These places have their own real stories to tell, more magical than we could have dreamed.

A Personal Pilgrimage

In Japanese culture there are two opposing poles. They may be called *omote* and *ura*, "front" and "back"; or *ken* and *mitsu*, "revealed" and "hidden." It's generally supposed that the "back" is superior to the "front," and that the "hidden" is higher than the "revealed," as these are where the mystery resides. In other words, things which are not easy to see, which hide somewhat from obvious view, are wonderful.

In 1971, essayist and doyenne of traditional Japanese culture Shirasu Masako penned a legendary book titled *Kakurezato* [Hidden hamlets]. This was the time of Japan's big economic growth when the modern tourism boom had just started. But Shirasu avoided the Golden Pavilion and the Silver Pavilion. She traveled deep into the mountains, visited temples nobody had ever heard of, and along the way she polished her insights into the essence of Japanese beauty.

I first met Shirasu in 1994 when we did an interview for *Geijutsu Shincho* magazine entitled "What's Real?" and from that time onward I learned much from her penetrating eye and sharp tongue.

In ensuing years, I traveled the country exploring remote places as I worked on projects to restore old houses. Beyond the demands of work, I made an effort on my own to follow in Shirasu's footsteps, visiting unknown villages and forgotten temples.

These days the towns and temples at the "front" of Japan, overwhelmed with tourists, no longer feel quite so special. And anyway, who amongst us doesn't harbor the thrill of finding a place other people don't know about, a hidden crypt which only you have yet penetrated?

From ancient times Japan has had a tradition of pilgrimage. For me, both my work on old houses and the visits I made to places Shirasu had written about were "pilgrimages" on which I made many discoveries.

With the aim of introducing some of the hidden places where one might discover "what's real," I embarked in 2017 on the project of this book. Journalist Kiyono Yumi and photographer Ohshima Atsuyuki accompanied me on these travels as the three of us went to faraway villages in Akita in the north, Amami Oshima island south of Kyushu, and Aogashima Island in the middle of the Pacific.

As it happens, there are two types of "hidden hamlet": those that are truly hidden, and those that are merely "forgotten." Among the places we visited were Hiyoshi Taisha Shrine and Miidera Temple, both located in Otsu City to the east of Kyoto, and the Miura Peninsula just south of Tokyo. These locations are hardly hidden. You can get to Otsu in just fifteen minutes by train from downtown Kyoto; a train from Shinagawa Station in Tokyo will take you straight to Miura in a little over an hour. But while rich with cultural treasure, for the very reason that they lie right on the doorstep, they're overlooked. You can travel to them easily, but nobody knows anymore how to unlock their secrets.

I remember my father teasing friends who had just returned from a trip to Italy, where our family had lived, and which he knew well. He asked, "Did you manage to visit Cinque Terre?" "Oh yes, we did." "Did you get to the village of Manarola?" "Oh yes, that was lovely." And so it went, down the coast, until finally he asked about one tiny fishing village, and they said, "We didn't know about that." "Ha!" he pounced, "You missed everything!"

Even seasoned travelers when visiting tourist sites can overlook something wondrous just off the path. It's happened to me many times, and then I wonder if perhaps I've "missed everything!" I'm asking of myself the same question my father asked his friends.

From here on we set out together on a pilgrimage. But first I'd like to remind us all of Shirasu's words: "When you find a place people

The ancient Cow Monument appears in Shirasu's *Kakurezato*

don't know about, you want to tell them about it. But as soon as you tell them, it's immediately spoiled. Such is the cruel way of the world."

I agree with Shirasu that it's a cruel world. So I'd like to request my readers: please enjoy learning about the places in this book. But please never, ever, go there. That's what I would like to say. However, it might seem unfair that I have visited these places myself yet forbid my readers from doing so. I should reword this request: please, before exploring any of these places, think twice, or even three times, before you go.

1
Hidden Hamlets
Minami-Aizu, Fukushima Prefecture

There's a saying *Ushi ni hikarete Zenkoji mairi* "Drawn by a cow to worship at Zenkoji." The tale is that an old lady, washing her clothes by the river, hung some fabric on a cow to dry. The cow ran away and the old lady ran after it. The cow wandered here and there, and finally when the cow stopped, the woman found herself at Zenkoji, the pilgrimage temple of Nagano.

The point of the story is that the apparent reason one has been drawn to a place may not matter much. Out of no special desire of one's own, one is pulled by the runaway cow of fate to one's true destination. One of these places for me is Minami-Aizu in Fukushima Prefecture.

A guided tour

In 2018, I was contacted by One Story, a company I've worked with on outdoor dining events known as "Dining Out," who asked if I'd be interested in hosting a tour of the town of Minami-Aizu in southwestern Fukushima. It would involve several advance trips to see what tourist resources were to be found in the area, and then planning the tour.

The words "guide" and "tour" have a bit of a bad name these days, conjuring up someone carrying a flag while herding a flock of oblivious travelers through a crowded tourist site. There's an idea common in the world of modern tourism that individual travel is more advanced and sophisticated than tour groups. But I've traveled as a guest on tours such as this in Bhutan and in Italy where I learned more than I ever could have done on my own. A well-done tour can be just as enriching as a good book. Although I had never heard of Minami-Aizu and had to look it up on a map to see where it was, I immediately agreed.

Boarding the Tobu Line from Asakusa Station

The jump-off point for traveling around Minami-Aizu is the station of Aizu-Tajima. It's the end of the line for Tobu Railway's Liberty Aizu train, which departs from Asakusa Station in Tokyo.

I boarded the train at Asakusa full of expectation. The name "Aizu," for many people, including myself, is associated with the pitiable last stand of the shogunal loyalists at the town of Aizu-Wakamatsu in the Boshin War of 1868 at the time of the Meiji Restoration. Saddest is the tale of the Byakko-tai (White Tiger Unit), a group of nineteen teenage samurai. Standing on a hill overlooking the castle, the young men (most just sixteen or seventeen years old) all committed suicide when they saw smoke rising from the ramparts and thought the battle was lost.

Aizu-Wakamatsu lies just an hour or so north of Aizu-Tajima Station, so I looked forward to a chance to see this site with such a tragic history. Also, along the way to Aizu-Tajima, there's a branch of the Tobu line going to the colorful shrines of Nikko, a place I've loved since childhood.

In 1964 my family moved to Yokohama. At the age of twelve I was fascinated by trains and used to enjoy exploring the areas around Yokohama and Tokyo. I especially enjoyed taking the train to Nikko from Asakusa. I would store up my savings, and when I had enough, I'd

Tobu railway line tracks in the snow

buy a ticket to Nikko and make a little excursion. In those days the government-owned Japan Railways line was rather plain, but the private Tobu line, with plush seats and wide windows, felt luxurious. I always got a thrill out of riding it.

With childhood memories floating about me, I naturally expected that the express to Aizu-Tajima would go through Nikko on the way. But at some point our train turned off onto another spur and it was clear there would be no Nikko. Come to think of it, over fifty years had passed since I'd ridden this line as a child.

About two hours out of Tokyo, around where Tochigi Prefecture gives way to Fukushima Prefecture, the view out the train window changed to an expanse of pure white snow. Back at Asakusa Station where I had boarded, early spring was coming on. It was still deep winter here. I had never thought of Fukushima as particularly far away, but now I realized, "This is the north."

Billows of thatched roofs

At Aizu-Tajima Station, my companions met me, and we drove from there to the old inn town of Ouchi-juku. With a fame reaching far beyond Minami-Aizu, it's a well-known tourist site. In the Edo period, this was a *juku* (inn town) along the old Aizu Nishikaido road which ran from Aizu-Wakamatsu further north, to Imaichi in Nikko. Its dramatic townscape survives today as one of Japan's best preserved juku.

The best-known thatched village in Japan is Shirakawa-go in Gifu Prefecture, where the extra-tall thatched roofs are scattered in a picturesque valley. Ouchi-juku, which started as an inn town, not as an agricultural village, looks quite different. No scattering here—the houses are neatly arranged in parallel rows along a central street that runs up to the foot of a small hill where it stops in a T-junction. From here you walk up the hill for a panoramic view of the town.

In the old days, juku inn buildings all over Japan were usually thatched, as we can see from old paintings. Only a few juku survive today, and mostly their roofs were converted to tiles along the way. A fully thatched inn town like this is a rare survival.

The old inn town of Ouchi-juku

Until the 1960s the city of Kyoto, when viewed from a high vantage point, was a vast expanse of tiled roofs—a sight of course long gone today. They used to call it *iraka no umi*, "the sea of roof tiles." You could call Ouchi-juku's rows of thatched roofs *kayabuki no onami*, "great billows of thatch" rolling in from the sea.

The town that fell asleep until the 1970s

Ouchi-juku's history goes back to 1643, when it began as an inn town on a branch of the road taken by the feudal lords of Aizu when they made their biannual trip to Edo, known as *sankin-kotai* or "alternate attendance." It was required that every one of Japan's roughly three hundred feudal lords travel once every two years to Edo. The lord would reside one year in Edo, and then return the next year to his home fief. His wife and heir lived permanently in Edo, as hostages. The purpose was to keep powerful lords close at hand so they couldn't cause trouble—and also to impoverish them with the huge expense of the trips.

And the expenses were huge. Even a minor lord might travel with up to a hundred attendants. Daimyo entourages moving up and down the main arteries were a common sight, called *daimyo gyoretsu* "daimyo parades." A major daimyo such as the Lord of Kaga (Kanazawa) Fief, traveled with up to four thousand attendants. For the lord of a closer fief to Edo, the trip might take a week; for a daimyo from Kyushu, it could last a month. It's estimated that for a largish fief, a single trip could cost hundreds of millions of yen (millions of dollars) in today's money.

The most well-traveled route was the Tokaido, a road that stretched between Kyoto and Edo, immortalized in the woodblock-print series *Fifty-Three Stations of the Tokaido*. But there were numerous other routes, notably the Nakasendo road, which also went from Kyoto to Edo, but far inland, over the mountains of Gifu and Nagano. Along these routes, juku inn towns grew up. The typical inn town looked a lot like Ouchi-juku looks today: one central street lined with inns and shops. Nowadays, only traces of the Tokaido remain, but you can still find a few juku in good condition on the Nakasendo and other branch routes.

That was the background of how Ouchi grew up as a town. It has been calculated that just one night's stay of a lord, his attendants and his horses (the cost of keeping a horse at an inn was double the cost of a person), could run (in today's money) to five or ten million yen (forty to eighty thousand dollars) for a single night. That would be enough to keep the town comfortably until the next year's visit. At Ouchi, as time passed, the lords took another route, and it no longer functioned much as an inn town. The innkeepers turned to farming to supplement their income, and by the late Edo period, Ouchi-juku had become "half-agricultural, half-inn." With new roads built after Japan's opening to the world in the 1870s, it was bypassed completely, and, left behind in the mountains, it became purely a farming village. But the imposing houses along the central street remained.

Ouchi-juku slept quietly for the next hundred years. And this is what saved it. The other juku in Fukushima Prefecture—and in most places in Japan—swept away on the wave of modern development, were utterly transformed and lost most of their historical appeal. In the 1970s, Ouchi was rediscovered and declared by the government a *Juyo Dentoteki Kenzobutsu-gun Hozon Chiku* (usually shortened to just *Judenken*), "Preservation District for a Group of Important Traditional Buildings." Judenken can be found across Japan. They're marked by the fact that owners are encouraged to continue living in the houses, and they can used for commercial purposes, such as tourist rentals or restaurants.

At Ouchi, after its designation as Judenken, the roofs were stripped of the tin that had covered them since the 1950s, and the thatch restored. The central street's tarmac paving was removed and replaced with packed clay. The old town revived.

A thatch workshop in an abandoned schoolhouse

I went three times to Ouchi, once in March with snow on the ground, once when spring breezes were blowing in May and once during the autumn leaf season in November. No matter what season, the town was always full of visitors debouching from buses in the parking lot near the entrance to the village. There were also plenty of private cars. Most of the houses have become soba restaurants or souvenir shops catering to tourists. The town has not quite reached the state of over-capacity that one could call "over-tourism," but it's a cause for concern.

A bigger problem for Ouchi is that of thatch. With over forty large-scale thatched houses to look after, this requires vast quantities of thatch and expenditure, and also people with the skills to repair these roofs. In Iya Valley in Shikoku, where my colleagues and I manage a group of eight thatched houses plus my own house, Chiiori, this is a perennial worry, as it is in the town of Ugomachi in Akita Prefecture which we visit in Chapter 4. And so it is across Japan, wherever there are thatched houses.

Within this challenging environment, we met in Ouchi-juku a man who has devoted his life to thatching. He's Yoshimura Norio, owner of the one of the houses on the main street which now serves as the soba restaurant Komeya. Yoshimura worked for years as a public servant in the town office, but concerned about the future of thatching in Ouchi, he resigned his position and became a roof-thatcher. He's now involved in a host of activities from passing on the skills of preserving and thatching old houses, to projects furthering local food and festivals.

When I went to talk with Yoshimura, he told me, "There's something I want to show you," and pulling me out from the busy main street into the snowy fields behind the town, he led me to a disused elementary school. We entered the school and walked down a long cold corridor. Yoshimura threw open a door, and inside the classroom a thatched roof the size of a small house filled most of the space. Around it lay bamboo, straw rope and thatching utensils. He had set this room up as a thatching workshop. "Here we can work regardless of snowy or rainy weather," he explained.

I've visited a number of towns that have focused on thatched roofs, but this is the first time I've ever seen or heard of a town installing a thatch workshop in an old classroom. It's a great idea, and one would hope that Japan's Agency for Cultural Affairs could fund similar projects around the country.

A "National Treasure" collection of old wood

Near Yoshimura's restaurant is Misawaya, another thriving soba establishment. Its owner Tadaura Toyoji is a key person involved in Ouchi's thatched houses. He is also a construction contractor, which often involves tearing down old buildings. He brought us to his storehouse located not far from town to see his collection of *kozai* "old wood." The storehouse turned out to be truly massive, with old roof beams and columns as well as floorboards and wall sidings, stacked two stories high down the length of a gigantic warehouse. He had gathered kozai timbers not only from Fukushima Prefecture but from across the Tohoku region of northern Japan. Tadaura explained that this collection began when he saw old houses being dismantled, and magnificent pieces of old wood simply being thrown away. It felt like such a waste.

We were awed not only by the sheer quantity of old wood, but its quality. Tadaura used kozai to build his private home next door to his Misawaya restaurant. But vast quantities still remain in the storehouse. Inside it, we saw huge slabs of *keyaki* elm, *matsu* red pine, *buna* beech, *tsuga* Japanese hemlock, *sakura* cherry, *kashiwa* oak, *tochi* Japanese horse chestnut and *icho* gingko. In present day Japan, keyaki is practically an endangered species, while kashiwa and matsu have been attacked by pests or cut down to the degree that you rarely see large pieces of these types of wood.

The wood used in old farmhouses was hewn by hand with a kind of adze called a *chona*. I've always felt that old blackened beams with the chop-marks of chona on them are a kind of sculptural art. They have the hand of the carver upon them, and remind me of the enigmatic statues of the seventeenth-century monk-sculptor Enku. Carpenters stopped chiseling beams with chona over a century ago as modern sawmills came into the mainstream, so wood carved with chona is an increasingly rare sight. From this point of view, the beams stacked up in Tadaura's warehouse could be called National Treasures.

Ouchi-juku is quite small. Its central street runs just a third of a mile (five hundred meters) and its population comes to no more than about 150 people. It's remarkable that in such a small place, two visionaries like Yoshimura and Tadaura should be active. And it's not limited to just them. During the eight-month span of my three visits to Ouchi, I was struck by the fact that on each visit I found houses being rethatched. One could see from this that many people are devoted to preserving this unusual town.

Red roofs and a rural temple

Each time I visited Minami-Aizu, I would embark on a trip of discovery into the countryside. My travels ranged from the village of Hinoemata to the south to Showa-mura in the west. While I do believe that Ouchi-juku is Japan's finest remaining thatched village, it's also a well-developed tourist spot. I'm always on the lookout for other untouched villages that the crowds haven't got to yet.

One thing you see as you drive around these parts is lots of tall tin roofs painted maroon red. With a distinctive thickish bulge to them, they have the characteristic shape of thatched houses. And in fact they are thatched houses. People simply laid tin sheeting on top of the thatch, as a way of protecting against rain and snow. Underneath, a dense layer of thatch as well as the structure of big columns and thick roof beams usually remains.

The culture of thatched houses is not unique to Ouchi-juku and can be found throughout the Minami-Aizu region, in fact through out most of Japan. The difference lies in whether the government has recognized the old houses as Judenken, in which case funds come available to restore them. If not, they draw no interest from tourists. Even local people may not realize that these houses were thatched to begin with.

The secluded village of Showa-mura consists of a group of such red-roofed houses. The roofs may be tin, but the houses and the village remain close to their original condition.

I found other hidden spots of interest during these travels. One was as we were driving slightly west of Aizu-Tajima Station, and we came across a small temple located across the rice paddies called Nansenji. Standing all alone amidst a great expanse of fields was a two-story thatched gate. It was a scene out of a rustic landscape painting. When I visited in spring, I found that the tall tree behind the gate was a willow cherry with long drooping branches, and in contrast to the snows of winter this created a pastoral romance.

Until this time, when asked which were my favorite thatched gates, I had always answered the gate of Honen-in Temple along the Philosopher's Walk in Kyoto, and the thatched gate of Iriki House in the little town of Iriki, Kagoshima Prefecture. I've now added the gate of Nansenji to make up my "Three Thatched Gates of Japan."

A village of magariya farmhouses

Southwest of Nansenji we made our second discovery, the hamlet of Maesawa. Like Ouchi, the houses here have been declared Judenken,

The thatched gate of Nansenji Temple, Minami-Aizu

and thanks to that they're preserved in good condition. But Maesawa is less known than Ouchi and so is still off the beaten path.

My guide on my visits to Minami-Aizu was the freelance writer Suzuki Satomi, and it was she who introduced Maesawa to me. On our first visit, as I was about to enter the hamlet, Suzuki-san stopped me, saying, "No, this way first." She led me across the road and up the hill across from the village. We climbed a narrow path through a forest of *sugi* cryptomeria cedar until we reached a point where we could see across the valley, and there, framed amongst the sugi trees, appeared the hamlet of Maesawa. This was the perfect picture of a "hidden hamlet."

Maesawa was never a juku inn town, and thus has the "scattered" look of a farming village. It's made up of a cluster of *magariya* (L-shaped farmhouses) gathered in a dale at the foot of the hills. The most prominent feature of Maesawa is its fifteen or so magariya, which are unusually unified in their structure. In 1907 there was a big fire and most of the hamlet burned down. The carpenters of the area got together and recreated the old hamlet, and thus these houses were built all at once.

Magariya can be found in other places in Japan, but their greatest concentration is in the north. They owe their L-shape to the cold climate which required that people bring their livestock indoors to survive the harsh winters. A typical magariya consists of a main wing, where the people lived, and an extension where the animals were kept. Found in greatest abundance around the town of Tono in Iwate, they extend to Fukushima, Akita and other northern prefectures. Magariya are part of the romantic folklore of Tohoku.

In Maesawa the locals continue to live more or less as they always have. One house has been restored as the Magariya Museum and is open to the public. When I hear of a house done up as a museum I foresee that it will be a bureaucratic showpiece. The Museums of Such-and-Such that you run across in towns all around Japan have usually been restored to a bright polish. Curators fix them up according to historical theories that may not have much actually to do with local culture, and manage them with restrictive rules. Not much trace of real human life remains. For my research I need to see them, but I keep my visits brief.

But the house-museum at Maesawa felt still, happily, like a real farmhouse. When I visited in March, with snow still piled up on the roofs and in the fields, the *amado* wooden outer doors, as well as the *fusuma* inner sliding doors had all been removed, revealing an airy interior with the wind blowing through it. Once inside we found a smoky fire burning in the *irori* floor hearth. "Ah, that smell!" I thought, with a pang, remembering back to my old house, Chiiori, in Iya.

Sitting beside the irori hearth was Kokatsu Shuichi, one of the members of the local Maesawa Scenic Protection Society. From the first step on entering, I forgot completely that this was a museum. Feeling as I had long ago when I visited with one of my Iya neighbors, I had a long chat with Kokatsu by the irori.

Kokatsu is happy that the hamlet was named a Judenken and therefore has been restored and is in generally good shape. At the same time, as the villagers age, more of the houses are being abandoned. He worries about the hamlet's future.

Rapeseed blossoms at Maesawa

Even knowing these concerns, Maesawa comes across as a little utopia. When I visited in May, the fields were flowering with yellow rapeseed blossoms. If I ever own or rent a house in Tohoku, I'd like to live in Maesawa. I feel a twinge of disloyalty to Chiiori, but such is the charm of this place.

Trees and heritage

I had gone to Minami-Aizu at the request of Yamazaki Takayuki who works for One Story, the driving force behind the "Dining Out" dinners we've done in Sado Island, Yazu in Tottori Prefecture and elsewhere. Yamazaki had been making trips on his own to Minami-Aizu, getting to know the key younger people in the area. He was trying to come up with a creative approach to travel in Fukushima's countryside, and in the end settled on the idea of a guided tour. But not an ordinary one.

In the tourist industries of Europe and Southeast Asia, there's a well-established genre of "cultural tours." Led by guides who have a knowledge about and love for the locality, they appeal to their clients' intellectual curiosity. They take them not just anywhere but to carefully chosen, one could say "carefully curated" historical sites, restaurants and lodgings.

One of the quirks of Japanese domestic tourism is that until recently tours of this type have hardly existed. It's been a matter of piling a lot of people into a big bus, showing them the official famous places and capping the day with a hearty dinner. The words "curated" and "cultural" aren't part of the planning process. However, it's not that Japan lacks the demand for such tours. There's a sophisticated type of Japanese traveler, well experienced from traveling abroad, who seeks more than just another bus junket. The industry has simply not caught up to the demand.

You hear the word *omotenashi* "hospitality" much used in Japan with regard to inns and restaurants. It usually refers to the thoughtfulness with which food is presented or the warm way that guests are welcomed. I would call a well-curated "cultural tour" a new form of omotenashi.

By the way, when I say "cultural tour," there's a tendency to think I'm talking about the wealthy, or museum specialists. But the travelers on such tours tend to be neither; they're people from normal walks of life who have a personal interest in culture or the natural environment. The tour doesn't need to be expensive or luxurious, and the guests come from anywhere.

In crafting a tour of Minami-Aizu with Yamazaki, we wanted to include themes which would ordinarily be lacking from a tourist package. One of these was "trees." The smothering of Japan's forests in *sugi* cedar plantations, much remarked upon in other chapters of this book, is one of Japan's more toxic modern systems. Minami-Aizu has a relatively low share of such plantations, and is rich in ancient trees. Coming here is a chance to "meet" some of them.

While temples and castles are marvelous, trees of several hundred years age are equally cultural heritage, although only rarely presented as such. In decades of guiding people around Japan, it's rare to see

The Great Gingko of Furumachi

cases where trees are pointed out as sights in their own right. People pass right by a gigantic millennial tree at the entrance of a temple, focused on the famous garden inside that they're determined to see. An example in Kyoto might be Shoren-in Temple. The towering *kusunoki* camphor trees with magnificent twisting branches that stand at its entrance, are Shoren-in's crowning glory. You could go to see these trees and not necessarily go inside. In fact I often do just that.

In Minami-Aizu stands an extraordinary ancient gingko tree, The Great Gingko of Furumachi, said to be eight hundred years old.

Yamazaki had found it on his travels and told me about it. According to an inscribed monument at its foot, the tree was planted in the Kenkyu era, which was around 1190. The trunk is 36 feet (11 meters) in circumference, and towers 115 feet (35 meters) tall. It being autumn, the leaves were turning from green to vivid yellow.

In the fall of 2019, we carried out our sample tour with a small number of guests. First we took everyone to see Ouchi-juku and Maesawa hamlet. Afterward we drove to the Great Gingko, which stands in the schoolyard of a closed elementary school.

In Japan it's not easy to see great trees like this. The mountains have been turned into "death forests" of dark sugi plantations, while towns across Japan are busy pruning off the branches of old trees, or simply chopping them off at the base. In 2021 it was revealed that the City of Tokyo would be cutting down almost a thousand century-old trees in its redevelopment plans for the Meiji Gaien district. All this to build a wider road and a shopping mall, in a city that hardly lacks either. But it does lack trees.

Old trees can still be found in the precincts of temples or "sacred woods" of shrines, but stands of really ancient trees such as one would see in European towns and villages are hard to find. The Great Gingko of Furumachi, with its freely spreading branches, was one of the treasures of the tour.

A country stage

Another highlight of our tour was the small outdoor stage Omomo-no-butai in the hamlet of Omomo. Nowadays, when we think of Kabuki, we picture the Grand Kabuki performed in big theaters in Tokyo, Kyoto and Osaka. But in Edo and Meiji times, that was just the tip of the iceberg of a vast network of little theaters that reached every corner of Japan. One can hardly overstate the degree to which Japan was theater-crazy. Hundreds of small wooden theaters still exist, many in remote villages, although most are now disused and in various states of decay. They used to host traveling troupes from Edo, and also staged their own local versions of *kagura* (shrine dance) and comic shows.

An audience of villagers at the Omomo-no-butai stage

Omomo-no-butai, rebuilt in its present form in 1895, has a rustic look, with a thatched roof overgrown by grasses. The stage is built in two parts, with a lower front section and a raised back section which is where the musicians used to sit. The whole thing is no larger than ten or twelve tatami mats (around 200 square feet or 18 square meters) in size, but its two-level structure is unique. I've never seen another stage like it.

For the tour Yamazaki-san arranged with the villagers to have them perform their local lion dance, a type of kagura shrine dance. When we arrived, the ground before the shrine was laid out with benches and folding chairs and a dozen or so of the villagers had gathered to see the show. The summer Kabuki had been canceled due to a typhoon, so they looked forward to this performance.

The musicians, holding a flute, shamisen and a clanging gong, took their places on stage, and were soon joined by a lion with a big red mask held aloft by two men. At first the lion's movements were slow and stately, but along came the comic *hyottoko* character, wearing a silly-looking mask with bulging eyes and a funny pinched mouth. The kagura dance proceeded, with the hyottoko making ribald jokes and riling up the increasingly agitated lion, which was hilarious, and had all of us in the audience in fits of laughter. These moments spent enjoying a rustic kagura along with a few villagers in the grounds of a country shrine, shadowed in trees—we were inside a Japanese arcadia.

The evening's dinner was held in a 150-year-old magariya farmhouse called Nanzanso. Thatch having been one of the themes of the tour, we wanted the guests to experience dinner in a thatched magariya. Since Nanzanso is not a restaurant, Yamazaki and his staff had to go to considerable effort to prepare the food and bring in everything, from cutlery to tables. We arranged for special lighting, and given the chilly fall season, also heating. A young couple from the town created a simple menu using food grown on ecological farms, which they paired with local wine and saké. And so ended our "cultural tour."

I was able to see Minami-Aizu in three seasons and learned something different each time. After the tour's dinner finale, I trained back to Tokyo on the Tobu line. Watching the scenery slip by, I started thinking once more about the tragedy of the young Byakko-tai samurai in Aizu in the Boshin War of 1868. And then it hit me: my plan had been to see Aizu-Wakamatsu and Nikko. But in the end, I never went near either of them.

Sea of Japan

Hyogo
Prefecture

Tottori
Prefecture

● Seiryuji Temple

Yazu

● Seitokuji Temple

Itaibara ●　　● Mitaki-en

● Ishitani-ke Mansion

Chizu

● Taru-mari

Okayama
Prefecture

2
Tastes of the Countryside
Yazu and Chizu, Tottori Prefecture

My work in Japan has been restoring old houses and helping local towns with rural revival projects. As a result I get invited to places hidden away in Japan's countryside I would never have seen in the normal course of things. What I've learned, however, is not always about how wonderful everything is, but the severe problems these towns are facing. And sometimes, the prospects for hope.

Since 2012 I've been involved with an event called "Dining Out" which takes food as its main theme. What happens at Dining Out is that a top Michelin-starred chef is invited to a remote place. There he devises a menu using only local materials, while bringing to it the techniques and creativity of modern high-end cuisine. Guests come from the big cities and enjoy the dinner at a banquet set in a beautiful venue, complete with lighting effects and a performance of local dance and music. My job has been pre-event location scouting, and serving as host on the evening of the dinner.

The event introduces urban gourmets to regional places they would otherwise not have known about or visited. However, the high-society guests are really just guinea pigs for the experiment. The project's true aim is to bring a fresh wind to regional hospitality.

In the field of hospitality, Japan lags behind Europe in its development of food in local areas. Michelin-starred restaurants abound in Tokyo, Kyoto and Osaka, but you would rarely find world class fare in small towns or fishing villages, such as is common in France, Spain or Italy.

The best food in the countryside is served in *onsen* hot-spring resort hotels. But what you typically see there is a highly baroque, at times even overwhelming feast: plates and bowls of every shape and kind arrayed with elaborately arranged fish, shrimps and various meats, herbs of the season and so forth. It's a glamorized version of the traditional kaiseki cuisine served in Kyoto. The focus is on color and variety—restaurants and hotels preparing this kind of food rarely go to much trouble to learn about their own local delicacies or figure out inventive ways to serve them. Much of the food is frozen, brought in from all over the place, piled up to create an impression of volume and luxury.

This fare pleased the domestic bus tours of the high growth era of the 1970s and 80s, and there are also plenty of foreign tourists today who enjoy the exotic color of it all. But there's a new Japanese traveler nowadays, and they are seeking less, not more. A few local ingredients that they may not have tasted before—combined in a creative way. That's enough. This was, after all, the original inspiration of kaiseki cuisine.

Since our first event in Sado Island, Dining Out has been held in dozens of locations across Japan. In 2018, we did one in Yazu in Tottori Prefecture. Until then, when I thought of Tottori, it was of the Tottori Sand Dunes or Mount Daisen, and I had never even heard the name of the small inland town of Yazu. As with other Dining Out events, we spent about half a year in advance visiting the town and checking out temples, shrines, farms and forests.

After the Yazu event was finished, the neighboring town of Chizu, which lies further inland to the south, invited me to visit them, and people from the Chizu town office showed me around. Like Yazu, I'd never heard of it. The question was, what could depopulating Chizu do to revive its fortunes?

When I set out on the search for "Hidden Japan," my intent was to seek out interesting places in the countryside, and then by writing about them, to draw attention to treasures that people had previously overlooked. I was surprised at the richness of Yazu and Chizu I'd glimpsed on my earlier trips, and so, wanting to learn more, in 2019 I made a return visit.

A shrine inside a temple

Tottori Prefecture is part of what has been called *Ura-Nihon* "the back of Japan." It preserves old legends such as *The White Rabbit of Inaba*, one of Japan's best-known folk tales. Its Shinto is influenced by ancient Izumo Shrine—the original, the "ur-shrine"—which is located not far away in neighboring Shimane Prefecture.

In Yazu, there's a Shingon Buddhist temple, Seiryuji, that enshrines the mystical Buddhist deity Fudo Myo-o. Inside the temple, behind the high altar, has been installed the worship hall of an old Shinto shrine, Hakuto Jinja (Shrine of the White Rabbit).

Seeing Shinto today, which has been mostly cleansed of all Buddhist elements, visitors to Japan, and even many Japanese, imagine that it was always so. But for centuries, Buddhism and Shinto had been bound in a partnership. Major Shinto sects, like those centered on the Hiyoshi, Tenmangu and Hachimangu shrines (each of these three boast thousands of shrines around Japan) were officiated by Buddhist monks who doubled as Shinto priests. All this was smashed in the upheaval of the Meiji Restoration in the 1870s when Shinto and Buddhism were forcefully divorced in a violent movement called *haibutsu kishaku* ("Abolish the Buddha, Cast Out Shakyamuni").

Haibutsu kishaku began at the instigation of the new Meiji government in 1868, with the goal of cleansing the nation of Buddhism, which was seen as "foreign." For a thousand years, Buddhist temples had controlled Shinto shrines. Buddhist ritual and beliefs dominated, while Shinto took a minor role on the sidelines. The Meiji leaders pulled Shinto out of the shadows where it had lain hidden for so long and raised it to primacy. Fusing Shinto with a new type of emperor worship, they aimed to build a new national ethnic identity which would also serve as military propaganda. In its most virulent form, haibutsu kishaku lasted from 1868 until 1873. During this period, thousands of Buddhist temples were destroyed and Shinto shrines across the nation were forced to cut themselves off from Buddhism. The campaign continued right into the 1880s, after which pressure was relaxed and Buddhism slowly recovered.

Nowadays the two religions keep discreetly apart, each with sharply different halls of worship, rituals and priesthoods. But here in the remote town of Yazu, far from the center, we find a Shinto shrine housed within a Buddhist temple. The old unity of Buddhism and Shinto is still unbroken.

Japan's original forest

Several miles south of Seiryuji, deeper in the mountains, is another Shingon temple called Seitokuji. We had chosen this for the venue for the Dining Out event. The old *sando* walkway to the temple features worn stone steps lined with maples and other ancient trees. Some of them are exceedingly rare, such as the *O-te-ue Icho* gingko which was planted by the Imperial Hand of exiled Emperor Godaigo in 1330, and a *kago-no-ki* laurel, also centuries old. These have been designated natural monuments of Tottori Prefecture.

The view up the walkway at Seitokuji is pure Harry Potter, a world of magic and mystery. This was what all of Japan's original forests looked like. Nowadays in most of Japan, the native trees have been felled and the slopes replanted with industrial monoculture of *sugi* cryptomeria and *hinoki* cedar. When old trees do survive in temple grounds or private gardens, they're truncated, branches lopped off, with the result that the fresh and lively spread of branches is lost. What we see is basically stumps.

As with the great gingko tree of Minami-Aizu, here it's the trees that are the important cultural heritage. When I see the primeval trees surviving at a place like Seitokuji, I'm moved more than by the most splendid National Treasures.

When I first came to Seitokuji Temple to prepare for the Dining Out event it was midsummer with sunlight streaming through the greenery. On our return trip it was late autumn, with a smattering of red and yellow leaves still clinging to the branches. The carpet of colorful leaves spreading over the old stone steps had the poignancy of autumn, and among the bare branches we could trace the painterly lines of old maples.

Ishitani-ke Mansion

Chizu, bordering Yazu to the south, lies deeper in the mountains. During the Edo period, the town flourished as Tottori's largest inn town, and in its center stands an enormous mansion, a nationally designated Important Cultural Property, called Ishitani-ke.

In many old towns of Japan you'll find one grand old house, usually built by a prosperous merchant or landowner, which stands above all its neighbors. From a house like this you can learn much about fine woods, furniture and carpentry, as well as craftsmanship of lacquer and woodcarving. I've seen dozens of such mansions until now, but Ishitani-ke is in a class of its own. The super-massive columns and roof beams simply awe the observer. Unprepared for what I was about to see, on entering the vast *doma* earthen-floored foyer, I literally had my breath taken away.

Among Japanese temples, Todai-ji (the Hall of the Great Buddha) in Nara takes pride of place for its massive wooden columns, 12 feet (3.5 meters) around and 150 feet (45 meters) high. While nowhere near this size, the Ishitani house is the grandest wooden house I've ever seen. You could call it the Todaiji of Japanese residential architecture. Of course you find bigger structures at temples and castles, but for private houses this is the largest that I know of.

The founder of the Ishitani household moved in the Genroku period (early 1700s) from Tottori Castle to Chizu, where he became a large landowner and

Calligraphy screens by Ichikawa Beian in hallway of Ishitani-ke

inn proprietor. By the end of the Edo period, the Ishitani family head had been appointed *oshoya* "Great Headman" of the town. After Meiji, when there was a nationwide hunger for good timber, they became known as *sanrin-o* "forestry barons," building up a fortune from forestry. This accounts for the astonishing size and quality of the woods used in the house, such as sliding doors made of single slabs of precious *keyaki* elm wood. In building this house, no expense was spared.

With such resources, the Ishitani family developed cultivated interests which you can see in the artworks displayed throughout the house. In the hallway, I noticed a pair of calligraphy screens brushed by Ichikawa Beian (1779–1858), a favorite calligrapher of mine. His crisp precise brushstrokes made him the ultimate model of the literati style. From this one piece one could judge the level of taste of this household.

Ishitani-ke's vast doma foyer alone is enough to make a trip to Chizu worthwhile, but the rest of the mansion's interior is also remarkable, with delicately crafted carvings over *ranma* door lintels, flame-shaped windows such as you would usually see only in a temple, and marvels of carpentry and lacquer craftsmanship everywhere.

The house was built up from accretions in different eras, with an Edo wing, a Meiji wing and so forth. The residential section, built in the Taisho era (1912–25) at the height of the family's fortunes, contains a Western-style staircase which, on arriving at the second floor, leads on to a bridge vaulting over a small atrium. From here you enter the private wing, which includes a room with a *kamidana* Shinto altar.

Kamidana are common in old houses, usually built in the form of a shelf raised up near the ceiling in the doma or the Buddha room. But they are usually rather modest in size, maybe twenty inches (fifty centimeters), or for great mansions, as much as six feet (two meters) across. Here the kamidana is a fully equipped Shinto shrine occupying an entire room. I've seen some large Buddhist altars before, but never a kamidana on this scale.

Most of the surviving old mansions, before they were restored, had fallen utterly into decay, to the degree that they have had to be practically rebuilt from ground up. Almost no trace remains of the lives of people who used to live in them. But until the Ishitanis donated this house to the township, this wealthy family had continued to reside here, in the splendor of a Japanese Downton Abbey, generation after generation in well maintained comfort. The house is in superb condition, and with its well-preserved architectural details and fine artworks, it speaks of the high cultural level achieved in Japan's countryside during and after the Edo period.

Kaiseki cuisine in the countryside

For most of my working life my efforts had been concentrated on the restoration of old houses and management of landscape. But the meeting with Chizu and Yazu arose from food. The Dining Out events opened my eyes to Japanese cuisine which I now see as key to rural revival. On this trip to Chizu, we made three discoveries related to food.

First was the inn-restaurant Hayashi Shinkan where we stayed in Chizu. They don't do any publicity on social media or restaurant websites, so until going there we didn't know what it was going to be

Dinner at Hayashi Shinkan

like. On arrival we were surprised to find that the inn consists of just three rooms. Each of them has a broad *tokonoma* alcove, and a private garden viewed beyond shoji sliding doors. In contrast to Ishitani house's muscular grandeur, this inn was built in the elegant *sukiya* style of Kyoto, with lightweight beams and columns, and delicate details. The house was immaculate, and the flowers decorating the foyer and living rooms were arranged with the subtle taste of a high-end Kyoto *ryokan* inn.

The kaiseki dinner here was one of the most austere, and delicious, I've ever tasted, relying on a just a handful of local herbs and meats. It was a reminder that kaiseki in its original form was reserved, almost stoic—a far cry from the fussy much-of-a-muchness of typical modern kaiseki. I recalled a dinner I once had at Wakuden restaurant near Kodaiji Temple in Kyoto. It was a snowy January evening, and they carried into the room a huge fire-burned Bizen-ware platter with one giant lobster on it, seasoned with salt. That was it.

As I indicated earlier, I despair at the sight of the usual ryokan or onsen dinner, faced with a daunting mass of delicacies spread wide in dozens of fancy bowls and plates. Modern kaiseki, especially in onsen and tourist resorts, has become the Japanese equivalent of the ancient Romans serving bowls of steamed nightingale tongues. Yet Hayashi Shinkan, here in rural Chizu, prepared a dinner at a level of sophistication equal to Kyoto's best kaiseki. Chizu is hardly a big tourist mecca, so one can only assume that this level of quality comes from something older in the tradition of this town.

The *okami* (madame of the restaurant) told us that the great-grandfather of the present owner had opened the town's first Western-style café back in the 1920s, the type of stylish foreign import that used to be described as *hai-karaa* "high color." The café was a sensation and people came from near and far to see it. Most small towns of Japan never had a hai-karaa café—we were reminded that Chizu had once been quite well off and even culturally avant garde due to the income from forestry.

Taru-mari bakery and brewery

These days, towns across Japan are competing to attract "U-turn" and "I-turn" young people to reinvigorate their declining communities. "U-turn" are young people who left and came back. "I-turn" are newcomers who came one way from the big cities. Chizu hosts a number of these new residents from outside.

We went to visit a bakery called Taru-mari, specializing in handmade bread using natural yeast. "Taru-mari" comes from a combination of the names of the baker Watanabe Itaru and his wife Mariko. They had originally opened a bakery in Chiba near Tokyo, but in search of the fresh unpolluted air needed for natural yeasts to thrive they moved first to Manabe in Okayama Prefecture, then to Chizu.

In Chizu they rented a disused former kindergarten which they renovated, setting up their kitchen and a café. While they began as a bakery, due to the focus on yeast, they expanded to making craft beer. They treated us to a tasting of their various brews, which were fresh, fruity, with the flavor of a light champagne.

Watanabe Itaru serving beer at Taru-mari café

As they developed their bakery, Watanabe and Mariko realized that they needed to go beyond commercial yeast to natural yeast cultivated from the wild. In their craft beer as well, they have explored the use of natural yeast. A third of the wheat used in their bread is grown locally. Secondary ingredients of beer such as barley, honey and fruits are also grown at local farms doing natural farming.

Herbs and a grassy roof at Mitaki-en

Taking our leave from Taru-mari Bakery and Brewery, we drove into the mountains northeast of the town center. After winding along the Ashizu River, we arrived at the secluded rural restaurant Mitaki-en, and this is where we had our third encounter with local food.

The area around the Ashizu River is mostly virgin forest, with huge old *tochi* horse chestnut and *buna* beech trees, and it's also well known for its maples. Mitaki-en occupies a large plot within the forest which follows the natural lay of the land. A thatched *minka* farmhouse and other old structures have been moved here. With one edge of the property bounded by a small river, the area is infused with fresh air and the tricking of water. As you walk on paths lined with mossy stepping stones, you pass wooden storage sheds, and glades with piles of tree branches where mushrooms are growing in the shade.

Former mayor Teratani Seiichiro created Mitaki-en in the years before he became mayor, and afterward he handed it over to his wife Setsuko to manage as okami.

When you arrive, you walk through an old worn gate, and what first strikes your eyes is a large house with a thatched roof that is totally overgrown with twigs and grasses. It reminded me of what my house in Iya Valley, Chiiori, looked like in 1973 when I first found it. Of course it's better to cut the grasses than not, but if you keep burning the *irori* hearth inside, the smoke dries out the thatch and coats it with thick layers of soot. The harm caused by the grasses is greatly slowed down. In a house with a burning irori, the sooty coating preserves the roof far longer than one would think possible. The house will be OK for a while.

Sunlight streaming through the trees around Mitaki-en restaurant

In modern Japan, even for thatched houses, there's a tendency to trim and polish everything. Mitaki-en is utterly different. Later I asked the okami Setsuko about the roof, and she said, "It's not that we're lax in tending to the house, it's that I love the grasses and I purposely keep it this way."

Letting grass grow in the thatch is not traditional—quite the opposite. It's more a modern sensibility, inspired by new ecological architecture. Recent years have seen experiments around the world with growing grasses and even trees on top of everything from private houses to giant factories. In Japan we see these grass-overgrown roofs in the work of modern architect Fujimori Terunobu. Here the okami-san is doing it on a small but touching local level. She's at the cutting edge.

The food at Mitaki-en centers on herbs and vegetables from the surrounding mountains. You can feel great pride in the making of it. In addition to tempura using mountain herbs, they serve their own homemade tofu, miso and pickles. The food was restrained, limited to a few choice dishes. The "plates" might be a chunk of wood or a strand of fern. We learned that the herbs used in our lunch had been picked that morning from the surrounding forest. This was food you could never taste in a big city, and almost never at your average *ryokan* hotel.

The mountains are covered with deep snow from December onward. We arrived near the end of November, and one week after our visit, Mitaki-en closed for the winter until the next March. We made it just in time to experience this remarkable restaurant.

Lunch at Mitaki-en

Mitaki-en is hardly an easy place to get to, but a constant stream of visitors come from all over the region. It's not just the food, it's also the sense and personality of the okami Setsuko that draws people here. Talking to Setsuko while seated at the irori hearth in the thatched house, we could see that in addition to her native charm, she upholds strict standards of cuisine—and she's a businesswoman.

The highly traditional Mitaki-en and the technologically experimental Taru-mari would seem to lie at opposite ends of the spectrum. But they share the same devotion to natural processes and handwork. In the natural yeast that Taru-Mari is so devoted to, and in the grassy roof at Mitaki-en, we can see a similar philosophy. In addition, Watanabe Itaru and Mariko, as well as Setsuko, know how to please customers and make their operations succeed as a business. They're models of rural revival.

An abandoned hamlet

From food we return to houses. Only a short drive from Chizu Station on the old Inbi railway line, lies the forgotten hamlet of Itaibara. This had been the main object of my previous visit with the town officials.

Itaibara lies in a small valley surrounded by mountains. The place is close to totally abandoned. Of the approximately three hundred houses in the hamlet, twenty are structures from the Edo and Meiji periods, and Tottori Prefecture has designated them as a *Judenken* "historical collection of old houses." This means that money can be made available for anyone who would like to fix up a house. But the people are gone.

Most of the village's narrow lanes are inaccessible to cars, and there's hardly any arable land. In the old days, villagers had survived on forestry and sericulture, and had not done much farming.

The hamlet curves along the bank of the Itaibara River, over which small bridges link it to the road from Chizu. Bordering the river is the Fujiwara-ke House, an attractive thatched house designated by

A lane in Itaibara hamlet

the township as a Cultural Property. In the house next to it, a young woman manages all by herself a café called Hotori. She came as part of a program to bring in young people, and she's on a contract of a year or so to take care of the café. Across the alley from Hotori, another young couple have opened a weaving atelier in a house in which they also live.

In Japan, the word *akiya* "abandoned house" implies a collapsing old structure in which people haven't lived for ages. But along the way to becoming an akiya, there's an intermediate stage, which could be called *han-akiya* "half-akiya." Many of the homeowners of this village have their main house somewhere else, coming back here only occasionally, some once a month, others once or twice a year at the Obon festival in mid-August and at New Year. Other houses are "lived in" by one old man or woman at death's door who actually resides in a nursing home.

In a process that occurs in rural areas all around the country, these houses don't get counted as abandoned, giving a skewed image of the true dire straits of such hamlets. As it happens, the han-akiya, recently lived in and hence in better condition, are the easiest to fix up—if their owners will allow it.

While this hamlet is one of the prides of Chizu, it's a source of worry. A few young people have moved into it, but nobody knows how long they'll stay; there are no shops and nowhere for visitors to spend the night. While the government has repaired some of the roofs, most houses are in various stages of decay, and the whole place looks sad and run down.

It's definitely a worrying sight, but for me, I feel only possibility when I see a place like this. Far removed from the busy world, this secluded village is perfectly suited to the country's priority policy of increasing tourism under the slogan of *Kanko Rikkoku*, "Build up the Nation with Tourism." Japan needs tourism, for both economic and cultural reasons, and it is a precious lifeline for many declining villages. But sadly, the focus has been on increasing visitor numbers, not on management techniques or the protection of cultural and natural heritage—leading to the sorts of "toxic tourism" that appear in this book. Itaibara presents a chance for a new kind of sustainable tourism that can revive dying communities such as this.

In the past, the fact that cars can't get into the alleys was a huge minus. But in the age of international tourism, it becomes part of the charm of the place. From the main road, it's just ten minutes to downtown Chizu, making it far more accessible than the hamlets of Minami-Aizu. As for the lack of agricultural land, which was a factor in the village's abandonment, it's largely irrelevant in this post-industrial age, when all you need is Wi-Fi.

The hamlet contains not only houses, but some quite large structures which had been *kura* storehouses or sericulture barns for silkworms. You could transform the houses into cottages where visitors can stay, while the storehouses and barns could become galleries and ateliers. With a little work, Itaibara would be counted as one of the beauties of the Chizu area and become a tourism jewel.

Italy also has an aging and declining population, and empty villages similar to Japan. Since the 1980s Italy has pioneered the concept of *albergo diffuso* "dispersed hotel" in an effort to revive its declining rural villages. In this system, there's one house which serves as the "front desk," while cottages for sleeping, and other locations for eating breakfast or dinner, are dispersed throughout the village. The whole place becomes one large "hotel."

When I was involved in a project to restore nine thatched houses in Iya Valley we used a similar concept, and it has been successful. I'm convinced that the desire among travelers to discover and stay at places like this is substantial.

On our trip, we found three treasures in Chizu. The first was food, as exemplified by Hayashi Shinkan inn, Taru-mari bakery and Mitaki-en restaurant, where local ingredients are valued and there's a respect for natural agriculture. The second was the Ishitani-ke Mansion. At present it's still hardly known outside of Chizu, but it's a powerful spot with international appeal. The last was the quiet hamlet of Itaibara, where the mundane world has been left behind, and cars can't get in.

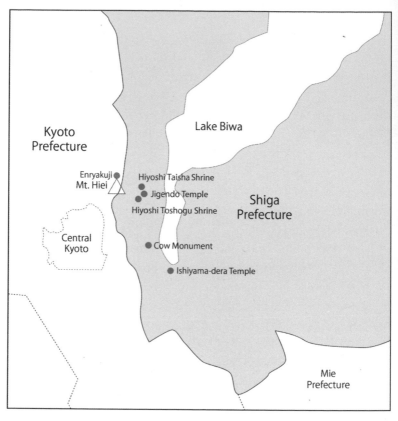

3

Shinto and Buddhist Stones

Hiyoshi Taisha, Jigendo, Ishiyama-dera, Shiga Prefecture

Hiyoshi Taisha Shrine in Otsu City on the shore of Lake Biwa in Shiga Prefecture lies just to the east of Kyoto. I live in Kameoka, to the west. My house stands in the grounds of an old Tenmangu shrine dedicated to the Shinto god of learning and calligraphy. I worked for decades for the Shinto religion of Oomoto in Kameoka, and used to act as translator for Shinto priests at international religious conferences.

I had long heard of Hiyoshi as one of the most important Shinto shrines in the country. Driving from Kameoka to Hiyoshi takes only about an hour and a half. And yet, to my embarrassment, while living for decades in Kameoka and a supposed Shinto specialist, I had never once visited the great shrine. So it was time.

On a cold March day, joined by my traveling companions, editor Kiyono Yumi and photographer Ohshima Atsuyuki, I set out from Kameoka, arriving at Otsu to find it drizzling and overcast. At Hiyoshi Taisha, the three of us were the only visitors.

Entering the grounds, the first thing one sees is the famous *sanno torii* gate which takes a unique shape with a triangular peak on the top. It's the hallmark of a whole family of shrines across the country, all of which bear some connection with Hiyoshi Taisha. The triangle bestows a "cosmic" feel beyond the simple lines of the ordinary torii,

The *sanno torii* gate at Hiyoshi Taisha Shrine

and this is not accidental, because it's a relic of the history of this shrine bound up with the Esoteric Buddhism of the Tendai sect, founded on nearby Mount Hiei.

In Japan, Esoteric Buddhism is called *Mikkyo*, which means "secret teachings," based on ancient Buddhist rituals and initiations. The word "esoteric" is simply a posh word for "secret." The earliest forms of Buddhism to enter Japan were all cousins of Mikkyo, with their emphasis on secret wisdom, and behind them even deeper secrets. The forms of statues, the implements on the altar, the sounds of the sutra chants, all carried numinous power, too awesome to be disclosed to any but initiates. The closest cousin to Japanese Mikkyo in Asia would be the mystical Buddhism of Tibet.

It's hard to see how Mikkyo mysteries fit in with a Shinto shrine like Hiyoshi. But when we speak of Shinto, most Japanese people would think of the systematized modern Shinto that grew up after the Meiji Restoration in 1868. Visitors from abroad would have no way of knowing that Shinto had ever been different from what they see today. However, Hiyoshi grew up in the pre-Meiji days when Shinto and Buddhism were still bound in a unity.

The great Tendai temple of Enryakuji at the peak of Mount Hiei in northwest Kyoto lies just up the hill to the west of Hiyoshi Shrine. It was founded by the monk Saicho in 788 after he returned from Mount Tiantai in China carrying the teachings of Chinese Mikkyo, which he called Tendai (the Japanese pronunciation of Tiantai). It has remained the center of Tendai Buddhism ever since.

When Saicho arrived at the mountaintop, he found it already occupied by several gods who protected the mountain. Saicho named them collectively *Sanno* "King of the Mountain," and enshrined them as protectors of Enryakuji. That was the start of Hiyoshi Taisha Shrine.

As Tendai, under imperial patronage, spread throughout the country, it carried along with it the cult of Hiyoshi Taisha. Wherever the Tendai Mikkyo Buddhas went, the Hiyoshi Shinto gods followed. Presently there are over 3,700 shrines across the nation known under varying names of Sanno, Hiyoshi and Hie, of which Hiyoshi Taisha is the mother ship. In Tokyo, the huge white granite torii gate at Sanno Hie Shrine, standing prominently on the main avenue in the Akasaka area, with its telltale triangle on the top, would be familiar to many people who have lived in or traveled to Tokyo.

People have interpreted the enigmatic triangle of the sanno torii gate in many different ways. Some say it's a *gassho*, Buddhist-style hands in prayer. Others say that it symbolizes the mystical union of Mikkyo's "Two Realms," the Diamond Realm and the Womb Realm. It reminds me of the mysterious pyramid with an eye at the top that features on the US one-dollar bill. Whatever its true meaning, all agree that the triangle of the Hiyoshi torii represents the unity of Buddhism and Shintoism.

A messy divorce

Tendai Mikkyo and Hiyoshi Shinto were tied together as husband and wife, but sad to say, marital relations did not always go smoothly.

Looking at Kyoto from the point of view of the geomancer's compass, Enryakuji Temple and Mount Hiei are located in the northeast. Called *kimon* "demonic gate," the northeast has traditionally been seen as the unlucky direction, and it was believed that wild and unruly spirits dwelled there. True to that belief, Mount Hiei, home of armed military monks who periodically descended into Kyoto and threatened the capital, was the source of strife for hundreds of years. Perhaps it was only natural that clashes between Enryakuji and Hiyoshi should take a violent direction.

When Buddhism first came to Japan, Buddhist thinkers needed to find a way to encompass the Shinto gods, so they came up with a system called *Honji Suijaku* "Original Essence, Dependent Traces." The idea was that the Buddhas and Bodhisattvas are the original and essential beings, while the Shinto gods who inhabit Japan are "traces" of these, local avatars. It was obviously a system that put Buddhism in a superior role. Based on this, Enryakuji controlled the Hiyoshi shrines for centuries.

In 1683, in the early years of the Edo period, the priests of Hiyoshi revolted against the Honji Suijaku doctrine, and declared independence from Enryakuji. They pulled the Buddhist statues and implements out from the seven Hiyoshi shrines and burned them. Before this there had been incidents of destruction of Buddhist sites, such as Todaiji (the Hall of the Great Buddha) in Nara burned down by military leader Taira no Kiyomori in the eleventh century, and Enryakuji itself smashed by daimyo Oda Nobunaga in the late 1500s, but those were campaigns of conquest. This is one of the rare cases of destruction on purely religious grounds.

The monks of Mount Hiei relayed strong objections to the shogunate in Edo with the result that the shrine priests were punished, and new Buddhist images and ritual articles were restored to the shrines. The grudge of the shrine priests went underground, resurfacing two hundred years later in 1868 at the time of the *haibutsu kishaku* ("Abolish the Buddha, Cast Out Shakyamuni") movement in early Meiji.

At Hiyoshi, this took an especially violent form as the Shinto priests dragged Buddhist statues and religious objects out of the shrines and trashed them all. It's recorded that over a thousand religious artifacts were destroyed at the time. Even the triangle on the top of the sanno torii gate was problematic and removed for a while until finally put back in 1915.[1]

As we walked under the torii, alone in the drizzle, all about us seemed supremely peaceful and quiet. The torii, symbolizing the unity of Shinto and Buddhism, seemed to whisper of deep esoteric philosophy that we could only guess of. But behind it all lay a fierce history of grudge and divorce.

Cedar-bark roofing

We proceeded into the grounds. There are numerous shrine buildings scattered over a wide area, so it's hard to get one's bearings. Altogether there are forty-some structures gathered into two wings of the shrine precincts: the Higashi Hongu "Eastern Shrine" and Nishi Hongu "Western Shrine."

We set our course to the Eastern Shrine. After passing through an impressive gate, we found ourselves facing a group of shrine buildings with gently sloping *hiwada-buki* cedar-bark roofs. A common sight in Kyoto palaces and religious places with high cachet, hiwada-buki is made by overlaying thousands of thin strips of cedar bark. It makes a dense laminate which is more durable than thatch, lasting up to a century.

Hiwada-buki is a common sight in Japan, found in many locations from small shrines to the grand Kiyomizu Temple in Kyoto. But in fact it is unique in the world. Thatch made from leaves, reeds and grasses can be found in many countries, as well as roofs of wooden shingles. But hiwada-buki—a laminate made of strips of bark—is a Japanese native invention with hardly any counterpart elsewhere. While it seems to have existed as early as the seventh century, it came into its own in the Heian period. That's when Japan first became aware of itself. As the Heian court nobles settled into their life of aristocratic grace in Kyoto, the distinction began to be made between *karayo* "Chinese style" and *wayo* "Japanese style."

---

1. Cf: Breen, John and Teeuwen, Mark, *A New History of Shinto*, Wiley-Blackwell, Chichester, UK, 2010, pp. 94–98; pp. 108–109

Karayo is forceful, official, masculine, classical, continental. Wayo is gentle, feminine, elegant, private, "Japanese." The yin-and-yang division of karayo and wayo has echoed down the centuries to this day, impacting everything from calligraphy to ceramics. In architecture, karayo was glazed Chinese-style tiles; wayo was hiwada-buki cedar-bark roofing.

Hiwada-buki fit in well with the courtly sensibility of Heian, for which neither thatch nor ceramic tiles would do. Thatch by nature is thick and bushy, with a primitive earthy quality that made it ideal for the mood of mystical antiquity at Ise Grand Shrine, one of Shinto's holiest sites. However, for palaces and other kinds of shrines, thatch was a little too rustic—plus, it didn't last long. That's why the Ise shrines had to be rebuilt every twenty years—a tradition that still continues today. Chunky Chinese-style roof tiles were durable but could never achieve the same fine and subtle lines the aristocrats admired. By the end of the Heian era (794–1185), hiwada-buki came to be the preferred roofing of palaces and shrines.

At Hiyoshi they take hiwada-buki very seriously, to the extent that they exhibit in the grounds a cross-section of a shrine roof to show how hiwada-buki is made. Despite living in Japan for close to half a century, and having seen hundreds of such roofs, until visiting Hiyoshi I had no concept of how these roofs are actually put together.

Hiwada-buki might be the world's first laminated wood. It's lightweight, and in the case of a palace roof, the difference between ceramic tiles and cedar chips could amount to many tons. I read recently that there's a fear that Nijo Palace in Kyoto could collapse in a strong earthquake. The roof in Edo times had been hiwada-buki, but at some point it was replaced with the black tiles we see today. That makes the palace dangerously top-heavy.

Being a thin laminate, a sheet of hiwada-buki can be bent and twisted to make all kinds of curving shapes. You can do things with hiwada-buki that can be done with no other material. For Shinto, this allowed for experimentation. At Hiyoshi we see a classically reserved version. But in later years, shrine roofs around Japan stretched, rippled and billowed, as they piled up layers upon layers, convex upon concave, leading to truly baroque complications such as at Kitano-Tenmangu in Kyoto or Okayama's Kibitsu Shrine.

Thinking about the Momoyama era

The buildings in Hiyoshi's Eastern Shrine complex have a particularly graceful feel to them. While there are plenty of hiwada-buki structures in Kyoto, they mostly don't quite achieve this elegance. One senses something different here.

It goes back to Oda Nobunaga's assault on Mount Hiei in 1571. It was one of the last great atrocities of the century-long age of warfare that had riven Japan since the 1460s. Nobunaga had set himself the goal of unifying Japan, and when he found that the armed monks of Mount Hiei stood in his way, he didn't hesitate to attack. His army wiped out Enryakuji, burning all its temples and massacring hundreds of monks, all in the space of one night. In the process his troops also destroyed all the shrines of Hiyoshi.

Roofs at Hiyoshi Taisha Shrine

The shrine grounds were later restored by Nobunaga's successor Toyotomi Hideyoshi in the last years of the sixteenth century. That is to say, these shrine edifices were built at the very height of the flowering of Momoyama-era grandeur.

When speaking of Japanese art, "Momoyama" is a word tinged with glamour. It's the colorful era after the wars at the end of the Muromachi period, when Nobunaga and Hideyoshi ruled a newly unified Japan (1573–1603). "Momoyama" is actually an abbreviation of "Azuchi-Momoyama," referring to Nobunaga's Azuchi Castle and Hideyoshi's Momoyama Castle. Both of these gorgeous castles disappeared long ago, but they've lent their names to the era.

In the Momoyama period, newly enriched warlords hankered after the noblesse of Kyoto aristocracy, and they had the means to build on a scale never seen before. The country was largely at peace, and there was an explosion of artistic creativity. Momoyama only ran for about thirty years at the end of the sixteenth century, but it's a seminal time, like the High Renaissance was in the West—a few decades in which the forms that would be followed for centuries were invented.

It was a time of exuberance. Momoyama things are "big": castles with soaring towers, paintings done in broad strokes, kimono patterns with dash and flair. Momoyama art has energy and panache. At the same time, the artists looked back to the refined taste of Kyoto's court nobles, which called for elegance and restraint. In those few decades of the late 1500s, these two qualities—panache and delicacy—merged, creating the unique flavor of Momoyama. For tea ceremony, shrine

Wooden *komainu* lion dogs at Hiyoshi Taisha Shrine

and palace architecture, painting and much more, Momoyama is to this day the touchstone.

There are Momoyama buildings to be found in Kyoto proper, but mostly they consist of a single building here or there. A unified group like the one at Hiyoshi Taisha is rare.

Momoyama touches can be seen not only in the roofs, but the *komainu* "lion dog" sculptures which appear to be original sixteenth-century creations. You come across komainu commonly in shrines in Japan, but they're usually made of stone and situated outside near the entrance. These are wood, raised up onto the balconies of the shrines, where they're protected from rain and snow by the projecting eaves.

Exiting the Eastern Shrine, we walked west past other elegant structures, the Shirayama-gu and Usa-gu shrines, these too preserving that ineffable touch of Momoyama grace.

Invasion

But . . . once outside of the Eastern Shrine complex, Hiyoshi Taisha has been invaded by flashy metallic and plastic signs with bright lettering and eye-catching red arrows. Some are white and new; others, rusting debris in untended corners, are crumbling away. This is not unusual. It's what you would find at many, perhaps most shrines in Japan. Given Shinto's long tradition of shrine precincts being "pure" spaces, realms of the gods removed from the mundane world, it's a remarkable scene. In fact, the flood of trashy signage and other flotsam and jetsam that has invaded Japan's shrine precincts is one of the twenty-first century's intriguing cultural stories.

Outdoing the signs, at the entrance to Shirayama-gu, they've installed a chrome railing that one could only describe as stunning. Its zigzag shape, like something from a 1950s sci-fi movie set, shines with metallic brilliance amidst the brown and tan of the wooden shrines. Against this, the ancient buildings don't stand a chance.

All this has happened at the Western Shrine and its environs, as it did in many other shrines around the country. And yet certain Shinto holy places, such as Ise Shrine and Meiji Shrine in Tokyo, have maintained their primal purity and withstood the incursion of junk.

At Hiyoshi's Western Shrine, the magic circle has been broken. But some powerful charm still stops the signs, railings and the rest of it, at the gate of the Eastern Shrine. Beyond that gate, the shrines and pavilions are still intact, unchanged since the Momoyama period.

The outermost shrine

Most of the Hiyoshi buildings lie at the foot of the mountains, but on the top of Hachioji-yama Hill, which borders the main shrines, there's the Oku-no-Miya, or Inner Shrine. *Oku* can mean not only 'inner," but "higher," "deeper" or "outermost." Many temples and shrines have these, (called *oku-no-in* in the case of temples), often located quite a distance beyond the main structures, involving an exhausting walk— the pains you must take to penetrate to the outermost sanctum.

At Hiyoshi's Oku-no-Miya, there's a huge stone called Kogane-no-Oiwa "Great Golden Stone," flanked by two shrines, Ushio-gu and Sannomiya. Of course you can't see any of this from down below. We asked about how to get up there at the reception window at the Western Shrine, and were told it was a thirty-minute walk up the mountain. We hadn't brought warm clothes and the rain was growing steadily colder. So we gave up on the idea.

But with Hiyoshi having such a close relationship with the Tendai Mikkyo Buddhism of Mount Hiei, I found myself ruminating on the essence of the esoteric Mikkyo cult. Unlike the Zen or Amida Buddhist sects which are aboveboard and even in-your-face, Mikkyo is about secrets. You practice and gain initiation to a higher level, and then proceed slowly to even greater secrets, from *oku* to higher *oku*. Just seeing the main shrines down below would not be enough. Yes, rain or not, we would have to do it.

We started up the steps, but these were seemingly designed for giants, not humans. Dragging ourselves up them was a challenge. But we finally got to the top, and found once again those graceful Momoyama-period roofs on the two shrines raised high on the steep mountainside, on a framework of stilts similar to the deck at Kiyomizu

A view of Lake Biwa from Oku-no-miya, Hiyoshi Taisha Shrine

Temple in Kyoto. Far below us stretched Otsu City and the wide curve of Lake Biwa. These were truly "shrines in the sky."

Between the two shrines rose the Great Golden Stone covered in moss. It conjured the chthonian antiquity from which the Sanno gods had first appeared.

So far, I've given the meaning "gold" to *kogane*, but it can also simply mean "metal," such as silver, copper or tin. Bronze mirrors made of alloys of these metals are often treasured within Shinto shrines. The mirror is the "sacred object" through which the god manifests. The stone in fact had the shape of Shinto shrine mirror, covered in the moss of the ages. A mirror too large to be enshrined inside a sanctuary, and so instead it was placed here, in the wind and rain, to be guarded by the paired shrines on stilts.

It feels like the path doesn't really stop here. The stone is a great rusted doorway, guarding the entry to something even deeper and more "inner" than the Oku-no-Miya. Or is it a huge metallic eye? The impassive eye of a great whale, the Sanno "King of the Mountain," gazing imperiously down on the shrines of Hiyoshi and the lake below.

People love to talk of Japan as the "land of wood," but it would be no exaggeration to say that a visit to a shrine or temple is a meeting with stones.

On the way up, and on the way down, we saw not a single soul.

Hiyoshi Toshogu Shrine

In the early 1600s the most prominent abbot of Tendai Mikkyo was Tenkai, a crafty powerbroker in the style of a scheming Italian Renaissance cardinal. Tenkai skillfully steered through the political turmoil of the late Momoyama era, becoming a close confidant of shogun Tokugawa Ieyasu after he unified the country. Tenkai went on to advise later shoguns, living to be over a hundred. He helped to design the new city of Edo and in the meantime was involved in the rebuilding of both Enryakuji Temple and Hiyoshi Taisha Shrine.

The first shogun, Tokugawa Ieyasu, had expected to be buried not far from his castle in Shizuoka south of Edo. But at Ieyasu's deathbed in 1616, Tenkai claimed Ieyasu had desired to be enshrined according to a new Shinto religion, "The One Reality of Sanno Shinto" (Sanno, as mentioned earlier, was the name of the mountain god of Tendai's headquarters on Mount Hiei, which was worshipped by Hiyoshi Taisha Shrine). Tenkai seems to have made up this religion, which nobody had ever heard of before, especially for this purpose. After a period of struggle at the second shogun's court, Tenkai got his way: he had Ieyasu deified with the title of Toshogu Daigongen (*gongen* being the Tendai term for a Shinto avatar).

Tenkai then arranged to build a grand shrine named Toshogu in Ieyasu's honor. In the process, he maneuvered—even against the terms of Ieyasu's will—to have Ieyasu's remains removed from Shizuoka and enshrined instead at Nikko, far north of Edo. Afterward the Toshogu Shrine complex at Nikko became the mausoleums of Ieyasu and the early shoguns.

In 1623, in the midst of the Nikko arrangements, Tenkai constructed a small shrine next to Hiyoshi Taisha dedicated to Ieyasu.

Hiyoshi Toshogu Shrine

Tombstones at Jigendo Temple

It was done in a highly decorated mode called *Toshogu-zukuri* "To-shogu-style," marked by vivid carvings, bright painting and lots of gold leaf and gilded fittings. This became the model for the extravagant Toshogu shrines of Nikko which took their final form after this date, as well as other Toshogu shrines across the country, such as the Kunozan Toshogu near Shizuoka, and the small Toshogu which still stands in Ueno Park in Tokyo.

Since the Hiyoshi Toshogu was the original template for all the other Toshogus, it shouldn't be missed. But what we found waiting for us was another flight of stairs, this one of precipitously steep and impossibly narrow steps, which we climbed very gingerly in the freezing rain. We managed to get up there, only to find a closed gate. Peering through the slats I could see what had once been a colorful golden Nikko-like shrine, but it was clearly long unvisited, a relic.

Over this nearly abandoned shrine seems to float a century-old whiff of the anti-Buddhist movement *haibutsu kishaku* ("Abolish the Buddha, Cast Out Shakyamuni"). Part of the aim of this movement in early Meiji was to wipe away all traces of the Edo shogunate, which was thought to have usurped the rightful role of the emperor. At the

Thirteen stone Buddhas at Jigendo Temple

time, Tokugawa Ieyasu would not have been held in high regard at Hiyoshi Taisha, and it feels as if that mood still lingers. One wonders what faded grandeur might still be found inside the Toshogu's darkened interior.

Jigendo Temple

We descended the life-threatening stairs, and embarked on a walk around the local area. It consists of a number of Tendai sub-temples and abbot's residences nestled behind walls and gates, one of the Kyoto area's more attractive, yet hardly known historic neighborhoods. Our feet led us into the grounds of a sub-temple called Jigendo, and here again it was a meeting with stones.

The walkway into the grounds led through a moss garden set with an arrangement of stone lanterns with mushroom-shaped tops, fantasy-like, a scene from Alice in Wonderland. On reading the information placard, we learned that this was the temple of the great Tenkai himself. His posthumous title was Jigen-daishi, from which comes the name Jigendo.

Within the grounds is a marked-off area of several levels in which stand impressive tombstones. Reading the inscriptions, we saw Emperor Gomizuno-o, Tokugawa Ieyasu, and numerous other emperors and feudal lords. These stones are carved with artistic quality and in curious shapes. The other great esoteric center of Japan is Mount Koya (also known as Koya-san), famous for its sacred wood filled with commemorative tombstones. But the stones at Koya are placed rather at a jumble, and the quality varies, with "jade and pebbles mixed," as the Japanese saying goes. Jigendo is tiny in comparison, but its stones are aligned in neat rows, and they're carved with gemlike precision.

At the uppermost level we found a row of thirteen seated stone Buddhas. One glance at their weather-worn faces, and we could feel the air of antiquity. They sit impassively staring ahead, their bodies tilted at forward-leaning angles like the *moai* of Easter Island.

Looking into it later, I learned that they had been taken from an enigmatic group of forty-eight statues found in Shiga Prefecture's Takashima City, a few miles further up the western shore of Lake Biwa. They've been dated to roughly 1400. Nobody knows their origin. They're among Japan's most mysterious Buddhas.

The finely carved lanterns, tomb monuments and stone Buddhas of Jigendo stand in contrast to the massive, Jurassic Great Golden Stone at the top of the hill above Hiyoshi Taisha. Shinto is nature before the hand of man has touched it; Buddhism is civilization. The stones of shrines and temples reflect this.

The Cow Monument

The tombstones of Jigendo belong to a genre known as *kuyo-to* "memorial pagodas," with the word kuyo implying "service for the departed," or even "apology." The tradition of kuyo runs deep in Japan. Viewers of Marie Kondo's popular TV programs on tidying-up got a sense of this when they saw Kondo insist on a little ceremony of thanking each item that has outgrown its usefulness—a pair of old shoes or an empty box for electronics—before throwing it away.

It grows out of the belief in reincarnation. If you offer kuyo to the soul of the departed, you can help them to achieve a better life the next time around. From that, kuyo expands beyond people, to include all living beings, and in the spirit of animistic Shinto, even to "lifeless" objects, that are also believed to have souls. You see kuyo-to set up for discarded calligraphy brushes, used sewing needles and so on. In Tokyo, on the little island in the middle of Shinobazu Pond at Ueno Park, there are a number of these. There's one in honor of the turtles we've eaten, and another for disused eye-glasses.

In Shirasu Masako's *Kakurezato* [Hidden hamlets], an Ushi-to "Cow Monument" appears, dedicated to the spirit of a sacred cow. Since this too was in the city limits of Otsu, on the former site of a temple called Cho'anji, we decided to go and take a look at it.

In the old days the road between the old imperial capital, Kyoto, and Lake Biwa was known as Ou-saka, and halfway along the route stood Cho'anji, formerly Sekidera, the temple that appears in the famous Noh drama *Sekidera Komachi*. While it was once an important place, and the name Sekidera carries strong cultural resonances even now, this site is today hard to find. Finally we got there, which involved parking along a busy highway, walking on a side street over the tracks of the Keihan train line, and climbing up a hillside in the midst of suburban housing.

In these unprepossessing surroundings, there stood the Cow Monument, a fat stone pagoda in the shape of a big thick bottle. Its heft and volume lent it a certain gravitas.

The Cow Monument traces back to the eleventh-century Heian period. At the time, Sekidera, which had collapsed in an earthquake, was being rebuilt. Abbot Eshin, the monk in charge of the work, used a cow to help with the construction. The cow worked marvelously and untiringly, and got the reputation of being an incarnation of Buddha's disciple Kashapa. Starting with the great Regent Fujiwara Michinaga himself, the high society of the Heian court thronged to Sekidera to see the cow, until it became something of a great social movement.

After the cow died, the nobles set up this monument. In later days, this temple became associated with Ono-no-Komachi, legendary Heian beauty and poet, so some believe it to be her monument.

With its thick mid-section, it seems to me rather cow-like. But Shirasu Masako isn't convinced. She writes, "It suits neither a cow nor a beautiful woman—it seems rather to be the monument to a great person, perhaps Abbot Eshin himself."

In fact, it's the oldest and largest known monument of this shape. But one wonders, how on earth did they get this bulky monolith all the way up the hillside. Stones contain many enigmas.

Ishiyama-dera Temple

Leaving the Cow Monument behind us, we continued our pilgrimage, toward Ishiyama-dera Temple, also in Otsu. Speaking of stones, "Ishiyama" literally means "stone mountain."

Enryakuji Temple and Hiyoshi Taisha Shrine shared a similar fate to most of Kyoto, being burned down repeatedly during the two centuries of warfare preceding the founding of the Edo shogunate in 1603. However, Ishiyama-dera, founded in 747, was situated at some distance from the capital, and so suffered less from battles and fires. Remarkable ancient structures survive here.

The Todaimon entry gate dates back to 1190, the early Kamakura

The Todaimon gate of Ishiyama-dera Temple

period. Although altered somewhat in the Muromachi period, it still has the muscled power of Kamakura. The wide swoosh of its rooflines, like a great bird about to take flight, has the same feeling as the thirteenth-century Nandaimon gate of Todaiji Temple in Nara.

As one can see from the fact that I took such pleasure in the elegant roofs of Hiyoshi Taisha, I have a special interest in the roofs of East Asia. Ishiyama-dera's Todaimon gate and the Nandaimon gate of Nara both contain strong Chinese influence. At the time they were built, the roofs of Song and Yuan-dynasty China began to take a fantastical bent, soaring upward with a pronounced flare. The "winged roof" of Ishiyama-dera's gate is ascending upward toward heaven. Once you've passed through this gate, you've entered into a zone which is not of this world.

Ishiyama-dera's most distinctive sight is a great rocky outcropping, above which stands a graceful pagoda. The swirling wall of stone, over thirty-three feet (ten meters) in height, was created by overlapping layers of magma. The dynamic volcanic flow has been caught, frozen and then ripped into jagged edges by geologic processes. Stones don't get much better than this. Of course they would call this place Stone Mountain Temple.

Above the magma, the pagoda seems to float on waves of molten rock. It expresses the Buddhist concept of rising spiritual levels. We pass through the storms and turmoil of messy human life, to reach in the end a pure world above it all. The peaceful pagoda crowning the turbulent stone is a summing up of Buddhist philosophy

The pagoda takes a particular shape, known as a *tahoto*, a structure unique to Shingon Buddhism. It dates back to Kukai, the charismatic monk who traveled to China in the ninth century, and returned to Japan bringing advanced knowledge of esoteric teachings. He founded the Shingon sect and built the great Shingon center that still stands on Mount Koya, south of Nara.

Kukai appears to have learned of the tahoto form in China, although it's possible that he invented it himself. A tahoto consists of a square lower section, surmounted by a round plaster middle part, and

Tahoto pagoda, Ishiyama-dera Temple

above that a four-sided pyramidal roof. Each tahoto symbolizes sacred Mount Sumeru, center of the universe. A particularly grand one stands at the heart of the temple complex of Mount Koya.

This tahoto, donated to the temple by Minamoto no Yoritomo, founder of the Kamakura shogunate in the late twelfth century, is the oldest extant tahoto in Japan. Like the gate, also Kamakura period, its roof soars airily in four directions, but unlike the gate, which is tiled, the tahoto is *hiwada-buki* "cedar-bark" roofed. This lends it a particular grace. The original form of a tahoto may have come from China, but this one transcends China. As we saw with the roofs of Hiyoshi Taisha, there has long been a contrast between *karayo* (Chinese style), masculine and muscular, and *wayo* (Japanese style), feminine and elegant. This pagoda is wayo in its purest form. It could only have been built in Japan.

Pilgrimages

Ishiyama-dera is one of the Kannon temples included in the ancient Saikoku Sanjusansho "Thirty-three Temples of Western Japan." It's a pilgrimage route centered on the Kinki area (around Kyoto) dedicated to the worship of Kannon, the Buddhist Bodhisattva of Mercy. Shirasu Masako's book *Saikoku junrei* [Pilgrimage to western Japan] was written about her journey along this route, during which she visited Ishiyama-dera.

With my involvement with Iya Valley in Shikoku from a young age, I had always heard of the Shikoku Henro "Eighty-eight Temples of Shikoku" and assumed that it was Japan's oldest pilgrimage. It's believed to date back to the monk Kukai in the 800s. In recent years numerous books have been written about it, and it has achieved worldwide fame.

But it turns out that while the Shikoku Henro may have started with Kukai, the eighty-eight temples in fact only became established in their present form in the seventeenth century. Meanwhile, the thirty-three temples of Kannon have existed pretty much as they do today since the twelfth century. Which is to say, the Thirty-three Temples of Western Japan have a five-hundred-year head start.

In later years all sorts of pilgrimage routes grew up, such as the Thirty-three Temples of Bando (in Kanto, eastern Japan), the Thirty-six Mystical Sites of En-no-Gyoja, (a famous mystic and seer), and even outside of Buddhism, the Tour of Imperial Tombs, counting 124 locations in its entirety. All these show the popularity of pilgrimage travel in Japan over the centuries. There may be no other country with such a wide variety of pilgrimages that are still active today.

The impulse to set out on pilgrimage starts with the desire to gain spiritual merit. Beyond that, as we can see from the thriving traditional shopping and entertainment streets adjoining Ise Grand Shrine, that people added sightseeing to their sacred agenda. From quite ancient times, visits to temples and shrines had something about them of *Kanko Rikkoku*, "Build Up the Nation with Tourism," the government slogan of today.

With a last lingering glance at Ishiyama-dera's graceful tahoto, we wound our way down through the waves of stone, and back out the gate to the world of men. As we left Ishiyama-dera, twilight was just coming on.

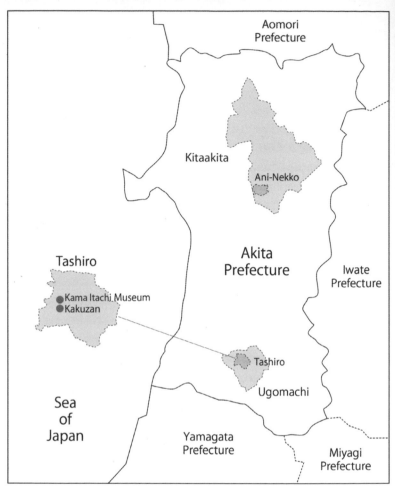

4

The Origin
of Butoh Dance
Ugomachi Tashiro, Ani-Nekko,
Akita Prefecture

The appeal of rural scenery would normally lie in details of local history or views of mountains and rivers. But my reason to travel to the village of Tashiro in Akita Prefecture had nothing to do with these things. It arose from happenings in Tokyo of the 1960s and 70s. And going back even beyond Japan, to France.

The 1960s witnessed a tremendous vogue for French literature in Japan. In it Japanese readers found subjects ignored by the mainstream of modern civilization. The French authors wrote about criminals, thieves, con men, homosexuals, transsexuals, the underworld of modern society. The novelist Mishima Yukio's taking up the theme of homosexuality with his book *Forbidden Colors* was one episode in this story.

Among these postwar French-influenced artists were founder of avant-garde Butoh dance Hijikata Tatsumi, and photographer Hosoe Eiko. In 1965, they took up residence in the small village of Tashiro in Ugomachi, Akita Prefecture, and there carried out an artistic "happening." It was documented in a photo book called *Kama Itachi* [Scythe weasel], published in 1969.

I've long had an interest in Butoh, and the haunting images in the photo book *Kama Itachi*. For this trip I wanted to follow the traces of Hijikata and Hosoe in Tashiro.

The birth of Butoh

Japan is the birthplace of Butoh dance, but the word Butoh is unfamiliar to many modern Japanese. While it's a quintessentially Japanese creation, it has grown far beyond Japan and today is better known in the outside world than in its home country. A fusion of Japanese and Western modernism, the Butoh style of dance is marked by an almost shocking elemental power. Before we talk about the village of Tashiro, we need to explore the history of Butoh.

Butoh is an avant-garde art form born in the early 1960s in Tokyo. Those were the days of the Ampo protests, when thousands filled the streets demonstrating against the US-Japan Security Treaty (abbreviated as Ampo) which allows America to keep bases on Japanese territory. It was a time of ferment and excitement. In the raunchy backstreets of Shinjuku, young dropouts from society gathered in bars and hideaways, while artists poured their energies into experimental works inspired by the dropping of the atom bombs on Hiroshima and Nagasaki. In the face of Japan's sudden postwar capitalist transformation, they asked themselves, "What really is Japan?"

The Butoh dance that grew up in this environment could be described as weird, grotesque, even disgusting. Dancers crept around the stage zombie-like as though infected with a dreadful illness. At the same time there was an erotic element, especially for the male actors who danced nearly nude. The women appeared in bedraggled lacy dresses looking like scary cast-off dolls.

Butoh is uniquely Japanese, but its creators had no love for traditional Japanese arts. Hijikata hated the weight of history, and was harshly critical of the frozen formal gestures of Noh and Nihon Buyo (Kabuki-inspired) dance. The Butoh stages, therefore, almost never made use of Japanese music; their soundtracks featured the Beatles, jazz and classical Western music. At its root was France after all, as in the raunchy works of Jean Genet. When seeking the "real Japan," early Butoh artists found it in a spattering mud-spout of criticism, anger and revulsion. Within this was cocooned a sort of distorted love.

Hijikata was born in 1928 in what is now Akita City. After graduating from the local technical high school, he studied German contemporary dance in Akita. Moving to Tokyo in 1947, he wandered around the capital, trying out various ideas. Then he met Ohno Kazuo, who would become Butoh's co-founder. Ohno was one of the leading avant-garde dancers of time, performing in a kind of torn and shabby drag. From this moment, Hijikata was launched on his new career. In 1959, with the blessing of Mishima Yukio, Hijikata performed what's now seen as the first true Butoh event, *Forbidden Colors* based on Mishima's novel, sharing the stage with a dead chicken and Ohno's adolescent son Ohno Yoshito. From that time Hijikata started calling his dance *Ankoku Butoh* ("dance of deep darkness"). Eventually this became abbreviated to simply Butoh. At some point, Hijikata took to covering his bare body with thick white powder, and this became the symbol of Butoh, copied around the world. At the premier of *Forbidden Colors*, foreign writers and critics were in the audience, and they helped spread the word internationally.

My first experience of Butoh was in 1978, when I was twenty-five years old. I went to see a performance in Tokyo by the Butoh group Dairakudakan ("Great Camel Battleship"), led by Maro Akaji. The grotesque and ghastly mood of that performance reminded me of the last scene of Richard Strauss' opera *Salome*, in which Salome kisses the bloody head of St John the Baptist. I made a cassette recording of this scene and sent it to Maro. I had no idea if Maro would actually listen to it, but when I went again to see Dairakudakan, sure enough this music was playing. But it had been cut up and altered into something shrieky and unrecognizable. That was Butoh.

It wasn't until after Hijikata death in 1986 that Butoh became an established form of contemporary dance in France and America. Ohno Kazuo's dance *La Argentina* in which he performed the role of an old and ruined tango dancer, swept the world. In Japan, Hijikata's students and his widow carried on his work. In addition to Maro's Dairakudakan, other world-renowned groups such as Sankaijuku remain active today.

Beyond the pass, the Kama Itachi village

From Kyoto we took the bullet train to Tokyo, and then headed north into Tohoku beyond Iwate Prefecture. From the nearest bullet-train station we rented a car, driving two more hours until we reached the town of Ugomachi. Getting there from Kyoto took over nine hours. At Ugomachi, Abe Hisao met us at his bookshop.

Abe is one of the directors of the small local Kama Itachi "Scythe Weasel" Museum. Following behind Abe's car we left the town of Ugomachi and set out for the village of Tashiro, driving up a winding road known as Nana-magari Toge, "Pass of Seven Turns." Reaching the viewpoint at the top we looked out over a wide panorama stretching out below us. From there it was another twenty minutes down to the village, where we found ourselves surrounded by a classic Japanese rural landscape of rice paddies and old houses.

Thatched houses were scattered here and there, and amongst the rice paddies we could see the distinctive Akita-style *hasa*, ten-foot (three-meter)-tall wooden posts. In the harvest season they line them with wooden slats from which they hang rice to dry. The place has likely hardly changed from the time Hijikata and Hosoe visited.

I learned about Tashiro from a friend, third generation Japanese-American Michael Sakamoto. Michael is a contemporary dancer deeply influenced by Hijikata's Butoh. He's also a photographer. Over the years Michael had regaled me with tales of Hijikata and pounded home the importance of Hosoe's seminal photography book *Kama Itachi*. Michael had visited Tashiro himself, and it was he who introduced Abe to us.

The reason why Hijikata and Hosoe chose Akita for their location was that Hijikata's father hailed from Ugomachi. During the war, Hosoe had taken refuge from the bombings in Tokyo by living for a while in the countryside of Yamagata. So the two of them were familiar with the Tohoku region

Fifty-five years ago, on a cold day in September, two unknown artists descended like a whirlwind on Tashiro, performed their outlandish poses and pranks, and then vanished as fast as they came. The

The road Nana-magari Toge "Pass of Seven Turns" leading to Tashiro

results appeared as black-and-white photos in Hosoe's book, propelling them both to fame.

In one photo, Hijikata, dressed in a skimpy white *yukata* kimono suddenly appears amongst a group of villagers, looking like an alien has taken a seat with them by the side of the rice paddies. In a blurred twilight photo, Hijikata wearing a long flowing gown, is seen in what ominously looks like a kidnap, whisking a baby away across barren fields. In one of the most famous shots, the near naked Hijikata, with his yukata flaring up over his head and wearing only a loincloth, leaps down from the roof of a storage shed, flying through the air before the startled eyes of a group of children.

Kama Itachi, the Scythe Weasel, is a ghost in old folklore who slices up travelers in the darkness of the night. So swiftly does he slash that the victim doesn't even realize he's been cut until a few hours later when the two halves of his body slip apart. Hosoe chose the title "Scythe Weasel" for his book as a metaphor for the psychological shock that people receive on seeing Butoh. Hosoe and Hijikata, appearing with the wind in the village of Tashiro and then flying away, were scythe weasels themselves.

View from above Nana-magari Toge "Pass of Seven Turns"

Japan's artists of the 1960s had been fascinated by French surrealism, which broke all the rules, reaching for a world beyond our daily normalities. By bringing grotesque Butoh, born in the urban jungle of Tokyo to the pure pastoral surroundings of Tashiro, the Butoh photographs made this extreme art form seem all the more surreal.

A Tohoku village

The Pass of Seven Turns winds over the hill and down into the valley, leading straight to Tashiro's grandest edifice, the Haseyama House. The Kama Itachi Museum has been set up in a storehouse on the grounds of Haseyama House. Inside are displayed photos from the *Kama Itachi* book, as well as other materials to do with early Butoh. It's a tiny museum, but for anyone who is interested in Butoh, it's an essential visit. Mr. Haseyama, descendant of the owner family, showed us around the mansion, which his family donated to Ugomachi, and the storehouse-museum. With the feeling that I had arrived at holy land, I took in its contents.

The Tohoku region of northern Japan is huge, encompassing the seven northernmost prefectures of the island of Honshu. One of these is Fukushima Prefecture, in which is the town of Minami-Aizu. At the time I was visiting Minami-Aizu I felt that I had come rather far north, but Fukushima is just at the lower edge of the northern prefectures. In Tashiro, we were in "deep Tohoku."

Tohoku is Japan's least known region, not only among foreign travelers, but even among the Japanese. Long seen as poor and backward, it was in fact the great fertile hinterland on which Edo based its wealth and power. In ancient times, it was the home of the prehistoric Jomon people, and later of the Ainu who were eventually driven north out of Honshu Island and up into Hokkaido. The farther north you go, the more you find place names deriving from Ainu.

The people traditionally have spoken a unique dialect which can be nearly unintelligible to someone from Kyoto. Some years ago I visited the town of Sakata on the western coast Yamagata Prefecture and met the local magnate who had endowed a university in the town and was involved in revival projects. When he spoke, with thick Tohoku *zu-zu* overlay, I simply couldn't pick out more than one word in three. My Japanese business partner from Kyoto couldn't do any better.

Ghost stories, like the "Scythe Weasel," abound. The town of Tono in Iwate Prefecture has a legend of *zashiki-arashi*, ghost children who live in a secret room of the house. In Tono, they actually built real rooms for these wraiths to live in and left food for them outside the door. In short, Tohoku feels "foreign" to Japan as we usually understand it, seriously different.

After his stay in Tashiro, Hijikata hardly ever visited Tohoku again. But Tohoku was always in his thoughts. If asked about the philosophy of Butoh, he would stress that Tohoku was his starting point, using the Akita dialect that he never shed all his life. When he talked of Tohoku, it was in terms of nature: "earth," "water," and "rice paddies"; and the innocent human community of the "village," living in thatch-roofed "houses," subsisting on farming rice.

But Hijikata's Tohoku had roots that are much deeper than the villages we see today. Even now, there hangs over Tohoku the air of the premodern Jomon civilization going back tens of thousands of years, and it was from that primitive lost world that Hijikata took his inspiration.

The Jomon period ran from roughly 14,000–300 BCE. Today, the thrust of practically everything we think of "Japanese" comes from Kansai (Kyoto/Osaka) and Edo (now Tokyo). But long before tea ceremony and Zen, before Buddhism, and even Shinto, there was the culture of the prehistoric Jomon people who lived on these islands for countless millennia. While officially ending in 300 BCE, the Jomon world finally faded away only in the fifth and sixth centuries AD with the advent of rice culture brought to Japan from the Asian continent.

If you go back to prehistory you find that Japan's deepest strata actually lie far away from Kyoto, in the cold and inhospitable north. The richest Jomon sites are to be found from Nagano up to Hokkaido. Here, for fourteen millennia—that is, about 95 percent of its entire history—was the real center of Japan.

One wonders, "Where did the Jomon people go?" The answer must be that they're still with us, living in Tohoku. One senses, as Hijikata did, that the people of Akita preserve some sort of deep ancestral knowledge. This lends a place like Ugomachi a certain mystique.

Jomon excavations have turned up a bewildering variety of earthenware objects: vessels decorated with whorls of rope patterns or jagged flame-like flanges, as well as figurines with distorted mask-like faces. The earthenware artifacts are endlessly inventive, and also utterly zany and outrageous. They might as well come from another planet compared to the ever-so-refined world of the Heian era and tea ceremony. Even more bizarre are the Jomon-era *dogu* clay figurines, in which we find baffling images of bearded gods with many breasts, idols with heart-heads and triangle-heads, and much more. From the point of view of later Japanese aesthetics, Jomon art is crude, profoundly unsettling. Inventive, zany, outrageous, baffling, crude, unsettling—that's Butoh.

Perhaps Hijikata did indeed reach far enough down into the well to pull up some ancient Jomon water. Sadly, I couldn't do that. The fact

above: Jomon vessel
(Photo: Tokyo National Museum)

left: Jomon *dogu* clay figurine
(Photo: Metropolitan Museum,
New York)

is that our visit to Tashiro was simply too short to probe the mystery. That's part of the story of *Hidden Japan*, since all of our visits were brief. At each town or temple, we could only peek behind the veil. This book is simply a collection of peeks.

On the other hand, maybe one shouldn't make too much of the Jomon-ness of a village like Tashiro. Most of what Hijikata and Hosoe experienced, and I later saw, was simply generic old Japanese village life: rice paddies, thatched houses, local herbs, villagers sitting in the fields, children playing.

My starting point as an adult in Japan was in the mountain village of Iya Valley in Shikoku in 1971. Later I wrote a thesis in college about Iya under the guidance of Professor John Hall, who had written a classic book in 1959 called *Village Japan*, describing life in a village in Okayama Prefecture. The village life that I and John Hall witnessed seemed close to eternal, something that had always been there, and with some changes always would be. Nobody then dreamed that by the start of the twenty-first century, villages across Japan would be dying.

All of it, the rice paddies, the houses, the rural shrines and their festivals, the old communities—not only in Akita, but in Iya and Chizu and across the country—is in terminal decay. Some places will find a way to survive on life-support; many others will simply disappear.

Two things are replacing these traditional ways of life. One is the government-sponsored construction frenzy: roads, dams, municipal halls and so forth, which will keep going until the last aged grandmother in the last collapsing house expires—and beyond.

The other, going quite the opposite direction, is the rewilding of Japan. Everywhere you see rice paddies no longer farmed and covered with weeds, empty homes succumbing to rot and vines, fences put up to keep out feral deer and wild boar. As the speed of rural abandonment picks up, houses and fields will decay and the jungle will reclaim the countryside. As you travel around Japan, you can see that starting to happen.

This makes the still-happy, still-vibrant village life of Tashiro poignant beyond words.

Holy Land for Butoh and photography

After half a century, the book *Kama Itachi* is one of only a few resources to understand early Butoh, as well as a record of a vanished lifestyle of the people of the village. But we need to keep in mind the fact that *Kama Itachi* was the vision of photographer Hosoe. In fact, many of the poses that Hijikata did for the book were choreographed by Hosoe. The "pure Butoh" that countless Butoh performers yearn for based on the images of this book is an illusion created by Hosoe. As a photo book it's a twentieth-century classic. From this point of view, Tashiro is holy land not only for Butoh but for modern Japanese photography.

When Butoh performers come to Tashiro, naturally the first thing they want to do is to mimic Hijikata. There's a photo in *Kama Itachi* of Hijikata perched like a crow high up on one of the slats of a *hasa* rice-drying rack. He's gazing off into the distance. Nowadays metal snow-protection racks are taking the place of the hasa. My Butoh-dancer friend Michael Sakamoto had himself photographed striking a pose on top of one of the snow-protection racks. In other photos, Michael danced in the village dressed in a *yukata* kimono as Hijikata had done.

Michael Sakamoto, posing on a snow-protection rack
(© Michael Sakamoto MuNK Series, 2016)

Inside the Kama Itachi Museum, there's a photo of Hijikata posed spookily in his trademark white yukata, hands dangling at this side, like a sort of ghost. When I saw this photo, although I'm far from being a Butoh dancer, I couldn't resist standing in front of it and trying out my own ghost pose.

The village as museum

Across the street from the Kama Itachi Museum is an old thatch-roofed house. The son and daughter-in-law of museum director Abe Hisao have set up a lodging for travelers here called Kakuzan. This is where we spent the night.

That evening, as we sat around the *irori* floor hearth, we were served excellent local fare using vegetables and herbs gathered by Abe and his wife. One course, prepared by stewing a fragrant herb called *koshi-abura* into the rice, provided a taste I'd never encountered before. As the cold Tohoku night fell and we gathered closer to the warm hearth, Abe's wife told stories. Such as the time, not long after moving here to get married, when she had actually seen the *zashiki-arashi* imps who abide in this old house.

In Tashiro, Abe's Kakuzan inn is not alone as a thatched house. Dozens still remain. The Thatched House Map drawn up by the locals shows photos of twenty large L-shaped *magariya* "bent houses" such as we saw in Minami-Aizu. A study done by Ugomachi township in 2015 confirmed the existence of eighty-six thatched houses in the area.

In Tashiro, they don't rethatch the roof by doing it all as once, as we do in Iya Valley, but instead add new thatch piecemeal, repairing patches in the roof as they decay and leaving others to fix later. As a result, a thatcher can work on several houses simultaneously. In 2013 they repaired eleven houses; from 2014 to 2017, they repaired seven houses each year. Before this, in the three years from 2010 to 2013, Ugomachi provided aid from the town's budget to train two young thatchers in order to carry on the local tradition.

With the thatching program and the opening of the Kama Itachi Museum, we can see Ugomachi is experimenting with approaches to rural revival. At the dinner at Kakuzan, we chatted with several young people who have come to live in the village. Like bakers and brewers Watanabe Itaru and his wife Mariko in the town of Chizu, these are "I-turn" (that is, they've come one way from the city, rather being locals who left the village and then returned in a "U-turn"). They're here under the aegis of Japan's *Chiiki Okoshi Kyoryoku-tai* "Rural Revival Domestic Peace Corp" program. The Japanese government sponsors young people to move to remote areas and supports them for a few years while they settle in and figure out a way to support themselves.

But the reality is that Tashiro is a well-nigh forgotten place. There are limits to what can be done on limited local budgets, and one can see that the *hasa* rice-drying racks and the thatched houses are disappearing. It may be only a matter of time before the whole precious rural environment of Tashiro collapses.

Meanwhile, Butoh has moved beyond Europe and America, and now has numerous followers around the globe, from South America to Southeast Asia. Butoh survives in Japan, but it hardly enjoys the recognition that it did some decades ago. Unknown and unseen by the Japanese public and national authorities, a steady stream of foreigners like Michael Sakamoto come to Tashiro to visit the holy land.

For the travelers from abroad who are interested in Butoh, the visit to the Kama Itachi Museum and the walk by the hasa in the fields fills them with the devotion of pilgrims. Morishita Ryu, director of Keio University's Hijikata Archives, which collaborated in setting up the museum, urges us to look beyond the exhibits. "It doesn't stop with the inside of the museum," he writes. "Outside the museum, the whole village, with its spreading rice fields is also an 'art gallery.' The thatched houses sprinkled in the fields where Hijikata jumped and ran with abandon are 'display areas.' The village of the Kama Itachi is one great museum."

Shangri-la beyond the tunnel

In 2017 I was invited to speak at an event at Odate City in northern Akita Prefecture, where I got to know Colin Flinn, a young American who works for the local NGO Akita-Ken Tsurisumu "Akita Dog Tourism." The word *ken* 犬 "dog" makes a pun with *ken* 県 "Prefecture." Colin told me of a remote village called Ani-Nekko in which he had taken an interest, and offered to drive me there.

The village is in the Ani area, now a part of Kitaakita City, famous among railroad fans for the quaint local Akita Inland Transit Railway. Beyond the reach of the railway lies the tiny village of Ani-Nekko.

After Colin had driven for some time over heavily-snowed roads, we finally reached a small tunnel, just wide enough for one car. The dark tunnel, lit by just a few ceiling lights, felt like a portal to another dimension. When we emerged into the light, the snowbound village lay before our eyes down in the valley. It was the image of Shangri-la.

This was two years before the trip to Tashiro described here, and on this return journey to Akita, I wanted to visit Ani-Nekko a second time. So we headed north from Ugomachi. We only had to go from a village in the south of Akita prefecture to one in the north, so I had assumed it would be an easy drive. But Tohoku is a big place. Checking it out later, I found that Akita Prefecture is two and a half times larger than Kyoto Prefecture. The drive took a full three hours. We needed to recalibrate our sense of distance from what we were used to in Kansai.

But thanks to the unexpected long hours of driving, we made another discovery along the way. I hadn't previously realized the extent of it, but Tohoku has a thatch-roof culture much richer than I had imagined. At first glance you don't see nostalgic thatched houses because most of them have been covered with tin roofing to protect from the weather. But, as in Minami-Aizu, when you look closely, the roofs betray the typical high pitch and fat rounded eaves of thatched houses. That is, the tin has simply been placed on top of the thatch. Below the tin, the thatch and heavy-beamed structure of old homes still remains.

The houses of Tohoku are bigger than those in Kansai or Shikoku, and because of the heavy snowfall they're built with sturdier columns and beams. Many are two-storied, and often they have the L-shaped *magariya* extension for keeping livestock during the winter.

On my previous visit with Colin, the village was blanketed in snow, so that I only caught a glimpse of it as we exited the tunnel. This time it was a bright spring day with fresh green on the trees. The cherry blossoms had fallen a month earlier in Kyoto, but here in early May they were just coming out.

First, we paid a visit to Sato Tetsuya, head of the village association. He told us of the history of this place, beginning with the *ochiudo* "refugees" who had settled here eight hundred years ago. In dozens of villages across Japan, there are stories about ochiudo, survivors of the courtly Heike clan who escaped after their disastrous loss to the samurai Genji clan in 1189. They immured themselves in faraway hamlets and distant islands, hiding from the search parties who combed the countryside looking for them. There, protected by the remoteness and inaccessibility of their hideaways, their descendants lived on to the present day. The village of Iya in Tokushima Prefecture, Shikoku, where I have my old thatched house Chiiori, also has vivid Heike ochiudo legends.

To our surprise, it seems that at Ani-Nekko the ochiudo were from the enemies of the Heike, the Genji clan. Why Genji warriors would have ended up here is a question. Maybe one of the search parties, having got this far, found it too difficult to go all the way back, and simply stayed on. Or it could be that first the Heike came, and then the Genji followed them, and after that their histories got all mixed up. The key takeaway, when you hear a village claim that it was settled by ochiudo, is that, like Iya and Ani-Nekko, it sees its identity as a Shangri-la. It's a haven removed from the world, off the grid, a place where one could disappear and never be found.

A lost world

Ani-Nekko, located far from the mundane world, preserves old things long vanished from other parts of Japan. One of these is the local musical and chanting tradition called *nekko-bangaku*. *Bangaku* is an old word used by the *shugendo* itinerant mages who practiced mountain austerities. It developed into a kind of *kagura* shrine dance, thought by some to be the origin of Noh drama. The bangaku of Ani-Nekko is known for the high literary quality of its lyrics. With warriors as its protagonists, it features a strong masculine dance, accompanied by drums, flutes and the trumpet-like sound of blown conch shells.

On this visit we weren't able to see bangaku performed, but we learned from the young man who guided us around the village that he attends bangaku drumming practice, from which we could see that this tradition is still alive.

Not far from Sato's house, the village gives way to forested slopes, and at their edge is the small Nekko Shrine. After walking narrow pathways through the rice paddies, we reached the shrine, where I noticed a plaque reading Kannon-do "Hall of Kannon." Inside, on the altar, was placed a golden image of Kannon, bodhisattva of compassion.

The official name of the god worshipped at the shrine is the very Shinto-sounding Sukunahikokami, but the cult of Kannon flourishes right in the heart of the shrine. The thing is, Kannon is a Buddhist deity. Nothing to do with Shinto.

They told us that at the New Year there's a ceremony at the shrine to pray for rich harvests and freedom from sickness and natural calamities, addressed to Kannon. As described in previous chapters, there was a violent divorce between Shinto and Buddhism that took place in the early Meiji period. But here in Ani-Nekko, long after the *haibutsu kishaku* Buddhist oppression of the 1870s, the mixture of Buddhism and Shinto goes right on.

Earlier, we saw something similar in Yazu in Tottori Prefecture, where a Shinto shrine stands inside a Buddhist temple, occupying its high altar. Such things are out of the question in big cities where the split between Buddhism and Shinto has set hard and fast. It's only in far-flung *kakurezato* "hidden hamlets" such as Yazu and Ani-Nekko, that traces of Japan's old religious fusion can still be seen.

Dusk was coming on, so we drove back through the dark tunnel to the outside world. Colin had said that this tunnel is what made him fall in love with this village, and for me too, it was the dramatic entrance through the tunnel that had stuck in my mind.

Nowadays in Japan, an old single-lane tunnel would be seen as

Golden Kannon bodhisattva enshrined at Nekko Shrine

"inconvenient," and one can imagine that the time will come when they decide to broaden or replace it. But in this depopulated hamlet, there's simply no need for more "convenience." Rather than that, if you used the construction budget to bring in young people who would till the fields and live in the old houses, managing some of them as guest cottages, this unique landscape would revive and survive.

This village of fantasy, with its ancient bangaku warrior's dance, and a shrine where the Shinto god and Buddhist Kannon bodhisattva dwell in harmony, seems to have a strong life force dating many centuries to when the ochiudo refugees moved in here. I hope that future visitors, just like Colin and I, will approach through this tunnel, and when they emerge, see the same view of Shangri-la open up before them, to their surprise and joy.

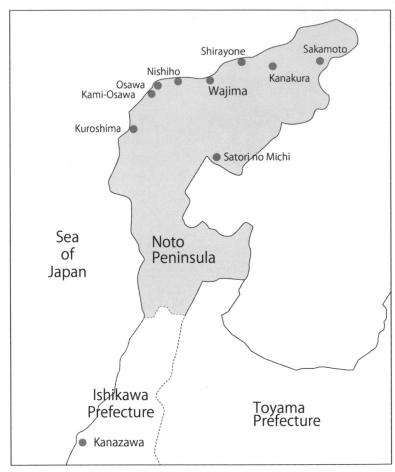

Shirayone

Sakamoto

Nishiho

Osawa

Kanakura

Kami-Osawa

Wajima

Kuroshima

Satori no Michi

Sea
of
Japan

Noto
Peninsula

Ishikawa
Prefecture

Toyama
Prefecture

Kanazawa

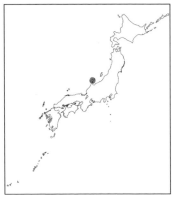

5

The Luxury of Nothing There

Noto Peninsula, Ishikawa Prefecture

Designer Issey Miyake is famous for his Pleats Please fashion line, featuring clothing items pressed into hundreds of pleats and wrinkles. A friend of mine in New York brought her beloved Pleats Please dress to the cleaners. But the people who did the ironing at the laundry didn't realize that the dress was supposed to be wrinkled, so they ironed it out as flat as they could. When it came back, the dress had doubled in length.

It's a favorite saying in Japan that "Japan is *semai*," meaning narrow or cramped. But that's only if you look at it on a two-dimensional map. In fact two thirds of Japan is mountains, and the coast is crinkled into myriads of peninsulas and inlets. If you took an iron to all that, Japan would likely flatten out to be as large as the continent of Australia.

I've been traveling around Japan for decades, and I find that Japan is in fact huge, and there are still hundreds of places I haven't managed to visit yet. One of these was the Noto Peninsula on the Sea of Japan coast. So I and my two travel companions decided to do a circuit of Noto.

For this trip, we were lucky enough to make the acquaintance of Takagi Shinji, an architect, house restorer and general authority on the cultural history of Noto. The peninsula projects like a long crooked finger pointing north and east into the ocean from the coast near Kanazawa City. The first place Takagi took us to was a small fishing village on the east coast of the peninsula, called Nakai-minami. It's part of the town of Anamizu, which faces a small bay. Takagi had designed a home here for Morikawa Jinkuro, proprietor of a *namako* sea cucumber business, to whom he introduced us.

The area around Nakai-minami is known for being a source of *kuchiko*, a snack made of dried layers of sea-cucumber ovaries. It's an expensive and unusual marine delicacy prized by gourmets, and I hadn't heard of it before. For a food lover, this sort of thing is irresistible. We sat on Morikawa's verandah looking out over his garden which faded into a view of the bay. While eating our braised kuchiko and boiled sea cucumber, we asked about the bay and its inlets. Afterward, Morikawa's wife, Yasuko, took us on a walk through the hamlet of Nakai-minami.

As is typical for fishing villages, the houses are clustered on a strip of flat land bordering the bay, backed by a ridge of low hills. On the hill sit temples and shrines, and here they're linked by a walkway called Satori-no-Michi, "Enlightenment Walk." We started out from Dairyu-ji Temple and then ambled through the compounds of Senkeiji, Io-in, Hiyoshi Shrine, Ichijo-in, Myo'o-in, ending up at Jifuku-in.

Grand sites designated as World Heritage are superstars to be admired from a distance. A group of small rural temples like this are like coming home to friends and family.

In old towns in Japan you'll often find a *teramachi* "temple neighborhood." Under the strict rules of the Edo shogunate, towns were divided into zones for samurai, merchants, temples and so forth. Usually they located the temple zone in the foothills or at the edge of town. The temples and shrines in a typical teramachi each represent different Buddhist or Shinto sects. You'll have a Zen temple, a Pure Land temple, maybe an esoteric *Mikkyo* temple, and sometimes a little temple devoted to Enma, Lord of the Underworld. Certain types of Shinto shrine, such as Inari (dedicated to abundant harvests and business success), and Tenmangu (dedicated to scholarship, where the village schools used to be) multiplied in their thousands far and wide throughout Japan, and would be found in almost every teramachi. Other shrines might be one-of-a-kind unique to the region.

Dairyuji Temple, along the Satori-no-Michi "Enlightenment Walk"

Kyoto's Tetsugaku-no-michi "Philosopher's Walk" is a famous example of a temple neighborhood where the temples are lined up in a row at the foot of Kyoto's eastern hills. In the old days, Enlightenment Walks existed everywhere in Japan.

At Nakai-minami's Enlightenment Walk, you see a range of gates and worship halls, some with flaring eaves, gilded fittings or carvings, and others quite plain and rustic. Each takes its place in a sacred sequence, like a prayer murmured with the turn of a pilgrim's rosary. From the bell tower at Jifuku-in, you look down on a panoramic view of the bay. When we visited in July, the walkway was lined with flowering pink and blue hydrangeas. A walk like this takes you out of the day-to-day, to ponder on religious faith and the beauties of nature. I find myself thinking, "These old towns really were very well designed."

A natural power spot

For our lodging that night, Takagi introduced us to Sakamoto, an inn-restaurant that he had designed, in Suzu City on the northeast

The entrance to the Sakamoto Inn

coast. Not wanting to be late for dinner, we pressed on to the northern tip of Noto, catching glimpses of bays and villages along the peninsula's eastern side as we went. As rural scenery began to give way to the busy township of Suzu, we took a side way, and after a bend in the road found ourselves at the entrance to Sakamoto.

The wide earthen parking lot and walkway up to the main house were shadowed by tall green maple trees. The branches interwove themselves with the sky, and through them the late-afternoon light leaked through.

Japan's gardens, flower arranging and other arts that make use of trees, flowers and grasses, are often described as "one with nature" but this is far from the truth. Rather they're "man-made nature," planned and manipulated to a high degree. Their interest lies in this balance between nature and human design.

It's a delicate balance, and in recent years, the emphasis in gardens and landscaping has shifted—away from messy unruly "nature," toward the well-behaved "man-made." Perhaps people have seen too many perfectly raked Zen gardens, and so they've come to believe that bare white sand is Japan's "nature." At a deeper level, Japan's modern culture is suffering from what I call "the victory of the industrial mode." The clean lines and reflective surfaces of factories and office towers, smooth white cement and shiny chrome—these things are seen as superior to the profusion of grasses, trees, vines and leaves that made up Japan's original jungle. In any case, the balance is being lost.

"Fallen leaves are dirty," is the angry call of urban residents demanding that unruly branches be drastically pruned, hopefully before the leaves even begin change color in the fall. For a more permanent solution, whole trees are chopped down and removed from urban centers. *Hagi* bush clover and *susuki* pampas grass, which symbolized the fall season and used to line roads and pathways, are cut down and replaced with tarmac. Pedestrian walks are paved with smooth concrete blocks, bordered with shiny aluminum guardrails, and around them is spread immaculate white gravel. In the process, we are left with the strangely flat, white and sterile Japan we see all around us.

And so, when I come across a place like this, where you can feel the love for untrammeled nature, my heart leaps up. The parking lot is made of earth. The wide verandah leading into the main house is open to the air, liberated. The annex next to a little pond has grass growing on its roof.

The main house, which was designed by Takagi to fit with the taste of the owner Sakamoto Shin'ichiro, features an impressive high-atrium dining room with an *irori* hearth and shiny blackened columns rising up to massive roof beams. It's a classic old farmhouse structure—but actually it's new, built around thirty years ago. The burnished floors and blackened beams are new wood which was aged by a lacquer technique known as *fuki-urushi* "polished lacquer."

Sakamoto is a culinary virtuoso. His father was a cook, and at a young age Sakamoto apprenticed under a French chef in Tokyo, and later studied cooking in Spain and Thailand. The evening's dinner was a quiet masterpiece prepared from carefully selected local fish, herbs and vegetables.

At the grass-roofed cottage by the pond, you can relax while drinking tea and listening to music. It isn't intended as a place for people to stay. But that night I got them to make an exception. I stretched out on the couch, and in the morning was awakened by light reflecting from the pool and the sounds of chirping birds. This is the environment built up and cherished by Sakamoto, so I can only thank him.

"Nothing there" scenery

On our second day, taking regretful leave of Sakamoto, we started driving west. Part of the reason for wanting to visit Noto was that I had seen a photo some years back of Wajima City's Shiroyone Rice Terraces cascading down a hillside above the coast. I take a special interest in rice terraces, so this was something I was determined to see. But on the way to Shiroyone we made a discovery.

It was the rice paddies of Kanakura in the township of Machinomachi. We found them by accident, when we noticed a broad stretch of green paddies off the side of the road. We turned in, and on the way we found a placard explaining that this is officially designated one of Japan's 100 Best Villages. That made me think twice, since the 100 Best This or 100 Best That are chosen by bureaucrats with political aims in mind, and when you see them they often aren't very special. But Kanakura lived up to its label.

Unlike the twisting seaside terraces we would see in Shiroyone, the rice paddies of Kanakura lie inland, in a gentle valley, and the paddies are wide and rectangular. It's not commented on—or even noticed— by most writers on Japanese scenery, but the nation has spent the last seventy years straightening out rice paddies in a government sponsored process called *hojo seibi* "agricultural land redeployment." Along with riverbank paving and mountain flattening, it's another item in the "construction state" menu. When you see a rice paddy you can immediately detect the difference: small irregular plots with curving edges are old ones; long straight lines indicate new ones.

Most of Japan's famous rice-terrace sites seen in photographs consist of the picturesque older type, curving plots like Shiroyone, often in cramped or steep locations. The "redeployed" rice paddies of Kanakura, in contrast, are wide and spacious, descending the soft slope of the valley in sheets of brilliant green. When we visited it was mid-July and the rice was at its most vivid, as if someone had laid out strips of scintillating emerald rugs over the fields and hillsides.

The old houses of Kanakura appear to be in quite good condition. We didn't see the usual visual clutter of Japanese villages: tin sheds, plastic greenhouses, blue sheeting, vending machines and prefab houses. There were no signs in bright red lettering, no chrome railings alongside the paths through the rice paddies. That is, it wasn't just that these were nice rice paddies; the charm lay in things that weren't there.

Scenery like this, with "nothing there"—without the tin, plastic, signage and other junk—is extremely rare in modern Japan. One could say that "nothing there" is the ultimate luxury.

With a backward glance, hoping that somehow this village will somehow manage to remain as it is, we left Kanakura for the next stage in our journey.

Rice terraces in the spirit of Issey Miyake

Finally we reached the destination I had been looking forward to, the rice terraces of Shiroyone. The flat spaciousness of Kanakura, with its broad rectangular rice paddies, has its appeal, but the truly great rice paddies are the old squiggly ones that flow over the landscape, following the natural topography of hills and valleys They're a hodgepodge of large and small with varied outlines; puzzle pieces painstakingly matched and inlaid into the mountainside.

The rice terraces of Shiroyone are narrow and eel-like, clinging to the slopes like the creases of a Pleats Please dress. When you put on one of Issey Miyake's dresses, it subtly brings out the lines of the body, and this is one reason for their enduring popularity. Likewise the terraces at Shiroyone, outlined by narrow footpaths between them, accent the flow of the mountainside as it descends. At the bottom stretches out the wide blue sea, making this truly an image from a painting.

Next to the terraces is a Michi-no-Eki "Roadside Station," one of the tourist compounds that have been built near sightseeing destinations across Japan with a big bus parking lot and an observation deck.

Shiroyone rice terraces

The buildings of the Michi-no-Eki are standard industrial, and from them visitors approach the rice terraces on a concrete walkway. Sadly, to tell the truth, while the Shiroyone terraces are indeed wonderful, the close proximity of the Michi-no-Eki makes the whole thing feel a bit staged. It's marvelous that these paddies still survive. But they've been absorbed into the business of tourism. On the other hand, while Kanakura lacks the striking view of mountain and sea, and its "redeployed" straight-edged paddies don't quite have the romance of the old irregular ones, the placid rural scenery, undisturbed by cars, buses, shops and the rest, is the place I would want to go back to. In fact, since this trip, I have gone back to Kanakura several times.

A few years ago I visited the ancient prehistoric stone circle of Stonehenge in southern England, thought to have been set up between 2000 and 3000 BCE. I couldn't help imagining what this would be like in Japan, where in the name of "convenience" there would be a bustling Michi-no-Eki right next to it, with parking lot, restaurants and souvenir shops. But I saw that at Stonehenge they had done the opposite. They put all the tourist facilities in a visitor center located a mile away. You leave your car there, buy a ticket and you can either be driven over a small road in a golf cart-like van, or walk to the site, which many people do.

When you arrive at the stone circle, you see only the mute stones standing amidst grassy pastures, and some sheep. "Ah, the mystery of thousands of years!" you sigh. After you finish, you can walk back or take a van, and you find yourself in the visitor center where you can have something to eat or buy souvenirs. It's cleverly choreographed so that the dream is never shattered. You're left with a quiet after-image as you ponder how and why the druids raised these numinous stones so long ago.

Thinking back to Stonehenge, I felt a little sorry for Shiroyone, where the terraces are among the most stunning in Japan. But I could be completely misreading it. Maybe a convenient parking lot right there—with a concrete observation deck from which you can easily snap a shot and then be quickly on your way—is just what people are looking for.

Wajima lacquer

Lacquer production centers can be found all over Japan, but Wajima, on Noto's north coast, is by far the best known. As I've collected Japanese art over the years, I find myself with bowls and trays that have been made in Wajima. When a special visitor comes to my house, we pull these off the shelf and serve dinner with them. The refined shapes and colors always leave a strong impression. Wajima was therefore a place I had long dreamed of visiting.

The first place that Takagi brought us to was Nushi-no-Ie, "House of the Lacquerware Merchant." Wajima was wiped out by a fire at the end of the Meiji period, and one of the first houses to be rebuilt was this one, a combined lacquerware wholesaler's shop and residence. It became the model for lacquer merchants from then forward, but by the 1980s it had been abandoned. In 1987, the lacquerware maker Wajimaya Zenni purchased it, and in 1990 it was totally renovated. Takagi was one of the people involved in the renovation.

You enter from a low waist-high door beside the street, and find yourself looking down a long hallway stretching from the *genkan* entrance through a narrow *doma* earthen-floored atrium. Along the side, raised up a level, is a polished-wood corridor, and again up another level are the rooms where people lived and did business. It's a classic *machiya* townhouse layout—but the finish of the sliding doors and other furnishings is like nothing else in this world.

In this house, the pillars, roof beams, floors, window frames, shoji lattices, all the way down to the water pump in the doma, every surface has been lacquered. The color is not red or black as is common, but a brownish liquid maroon known as *tamenuri*. It's actually a mixture of colors, typically created from a red lacquer base overlaid with semitransparent black or brown. Depending on how it was mixed or applied, it's sometimes more brown or reddish, other times it verges on purple. The tamenuri lacquer picks up the rays of light finding their way into the long dark hallways and reflects them with an illusionistic shimmer.

Our next stop was another place designed by Takagi, Quai Gallery. In contrast to his other projects, this is constructed with minimalist concrete, lending it a non-traditional feel, suitable to the modern lacquer works created by Wajima artist Seto Kunikatsu that are on display. Seto's works are simple in form, but they have a chic contemporary appeal. His slightly matte surfaces give a sculptural quality, which fit in with both old and new spaces. I couldn't resist wanting to buy some of his spoons and soba cups.

Sea cliffs

From Wajima, we drove counterclockwise around the peninsula, headed back south toward Kanazawa. What we found along the way was the cliffs of Nishiho Kaigan. After passing through a few fishing villages, our car started to climb a windy road along Noto's eastern side, and at a certain turn in the road we found ourselves overlooking a truly breathtaking vista. The road gyres on top of a sheer cliff, from where we looked down on waves crashing against the rocks below, glimmering with the slanting rays of the afternoon sun. As we drove

The sea cliffs of Nishiho, on the western shore of the Noto Peninsula

along we found view after changing view, to the extent that we kept stopping the car to get out and take photos.

The sad reality of modern Japan is that the sight of a seacoast not encased in concrete is a rare one. Nor is this limited to seacoasts. Even remote and atmospheric castle ruins are shored up with buttresses of shiny white concrete. The "ruin" is still there; the "atmosphere," not so much. This being the overwhelming trend of modern Japan, when I do find a seascape or river which remains untouched, it brings me a kind of bliss. The Shiroyone rice terraces made a splendid view, but the unconcreted cliffs of Nishiho are at least as good, and in any case perhaps rarer.

Behind a bamboo fence

From here we headed south, aiming for the *magaki* village of Osawa halfway down the western coast of the peninsula. Magaki is a kind of tall fence made of bamboo rushes that fishing villages would build on their sea side to fend off strong winds. As we approached Osawa, at the last bend in the high road we suddenly saw the little bay laid out below us, and curving along it, the magaki fences, and behind them the houses of the village. It was a truly dramatic approach.

I had seen magaki fences once before at the fishing village of Shukunegi on the south coast of Sado Island. At both Sado and here at Osawa, the fences are not the neatly woven low hedges made of bamboo twigs that we're familiar with in Kyoto. Here, they're made of tall trunks of raw bamboo, bunched together, lending them a rough primitive feel. At the top, narrow branches splay outward like a bamboo garden rake.

The Mediterranean has its notorious sirocco wind that blows out of the deserts of northern Africa toward Italy and Greece. This wind, which may not let up for weeks and can reach 60 miles (100 km) an hour, has been known to drive travelers literally out of their minds.

For some reason Sado Island and the Noto Peninsula, located in the Sea of Japan not so far from each other, are prone to sirocco-like winds. The magaki are built by villages that lie in the path of the gales, which in Sado is the south, and in Noto is the west. Seeing the magaki makes you realize that life in an old fishing village was not easy.

A few miles south of Osawa is Kami-Osawa "Upper Osawa," another magaki village. At the far end of its bay rises a sheer rock face, so the road stops here and turns inland, giving Kami-Osawa an "end of the earth" feel. Both Osawa and Kami-Osawa are designated by the Agency for Cultural Affairs as Important Cultural Landscapes. This is because not only the magaki, but the villages behind them preserve much of their original ambience.

Kami-Osawa is less tourist-visited and feels more artless than Osawa, and so it became my favorite. In the future if I ever set out to write a novel of the sea, I'd like to rent a house in Kami-Osawa and hide away from the world in this fishing village, writing in the morning and strolling under the bayside cliff at sunset.

The kitamae-bune merchant ships

From Kami-Osawa we drove to the old merchant town of Kuroshima on the western coast. The sun was slanting low by the time we got there. Kuroshima thrived during the Edo period and into the middle years of the Meiji era as one of the ports of the *kitamae-bune*, the merchant ships that plied the seas between Osaka and Hokkaido, running up the Sea of Japan coast.

Waves of thatched roofs at the old inn town of Ouchi-juku in Minami-Aizu, Fukushima Prefecture. After the feudal lord stopped traveling here in the seventeenth century, this village lay forgotten for two hundred years. (Chapter 1)

A perfectly preserved hamlet of thatched *magariya* (L-shaped farmhouses) at Maesawa in Minami-Aizu. (Chapter 1)

Thatched roofs overlaid with red-painted tin sheeting, triangular-roofed storehouses, green fields and gentle hills—rural scenery of Showa-mura in Minami-Aizu. (Chapter 1)

Magical-mystery steps—worn stones lined with maples and centuries-old trees on the approach to Seitokuji Temple in Yazu, Tottori Prefecture. (Chapter 2)

The vast *doma* entry hall of Ishitani-ke Mansion overlaid with gigantic roofbeams in Chizu, Tottori Prefecture. (Chapter 2)

A Shinto shrine used as the high altar of a Buddhist temple—a rare example of the old unity between Shinto and Buddhism, at Seiryuji Temple, Yazu, Tottori Prefecture. (Chapter 2)

The nearly abandoned hamlet of Itaibara, situated along the side of a stream. Inside are narrow lanes that cars cannot enter. Chizu, Tottori Prefecture. (Chapter 2)

A fairy-tale scene—grasses growing out of the thatched roof at Mitaki-en restaurant, Chizu, Tottori Prefecture. (Chapter 2)

Below is the turmoil of swirling lava. Above floats peaceful bliss. Japan's oldest and most perfect *tahoto* pagoda sums up Buddhist enlightenment. Ishiyama-dera, Shiga Prefecture. (Chapter 3)

Roofs of the Eastern Shrine, Hiyoshi Taisha, Shiga Prefecture. (Chapter 3)

"Alice in Wonderland" mushroom lanterns set in moss, at Jigendo Temple near Hiyoshi Taisha, dedicated to the crafty early-seventeenth-century Buddhist Abbot Tenkai. (Chapter 3)

Butoh troupe Dairakudakan. White-painted nearly nude bodies, weird poses, strange facial expressions—the haunting world of Butoh dance. (Chapter 4)

Long, dark, one-lane tunnel to the "Shangri-la" hamlet of Ani-Nekko, in Akita Prefecture. (Chapter 4)

Butoh founder Hijikata used to pose enigmatically on top of the *hasa* (grain-drying posts) at Tashiro in Akita Prefecture. (Chapter 4)

Emerging from the tunnel, Ani-Nekko sleeps under a blanket of snow. (Chapter 4)

Old-style rice terraces, irregular and clinging to the lines of the hillside, run down to the sea at Shiroyone, Noto Peninsula, Ishikawa Prefecture. (Chapter 5)

New-style rice terraces, wide and rectangular, shine brilliantly green at Kanakura, Noto Peninsula. (Chapter 5)

The surreal glimmer of the interior of Nushi-no-Ie "House of the Lacquerware Merchant." Every surface is coated with semitranslucent lacquer. At Wajima, Noto Peninsula. (Chapter 5)

Magaki bamboo fences erected to protect the fishing village from gales blowing off the sea. Kami-Osawa village, Noto Peninsula. (Chapter 5)

Katoku Beach on Amami Island, Kagoshima Prefecture. Called "Jurassic Beach" by the locals, it is the last unconcreted natural bay in Amami, soon to be drastically altered by the construction of large sea dikes (Chapter 6)

The branches of old *deigo* trees twist and writhe over a seaside walkway at Shodon hamlet, Kakeroma Island, Amami (Chapter 6)

Tsumabeni-cho, showing palms and butterflies near the beach, by Amami-based primitivist painter Tanaka Isson. (Chapter 6. Courtesy Tanaka Isson Museum, © 2022 Hiroshi Niiyama)

Seaside cliffs of hornfels, a metamorphic rock made up of alternating black and white stripes. At Susa, Yamaguchi Prefecture. (Chapter 7)

Outward-curving clay walls
in the old castle town of Hagi,
Yamaguchi Prefecture. (Chapter 7)

Karst outcroppings at Akiyoshidai plateau, Yamaguchi Prefecture, look uncannily like early Zen rock gardens. (Chapter 7)

Fifteenth-century garden, designed by the famed painter and garden designer Sesshu, at Joeiji Temple, Yamaguchi City. (Chapter 7)

Daimon gate, once part of Hideyoshi's legendary Fushimi Castle south of Kyoto, was donated to Miidera temple by Tokugawa Ieyasu. (Chapter 8)

Famed for its appearance in the poem cycle "Eight Views of Omi," the Evening Bell of Miidera appears in countless scrolls and paintings. (Chapter 8)

Nineteenth-century American art expert Ernest Fenellosa's grave at Homyo-in sub-temple of Miidera. Fenellosa was the precursor of the many collectors and writers about Japanese art who have flourished since his time. (Chapter 8)

Aogashima Island, while belonging to the City of Tokyo, lies hundreds of miles south in the Pacific Ocean. In the late 1700s, its inhabitants survived a volcanic eruption which left its mark in the double caldera in the center. Surrounded by forbidding cliffs, it's one of the hardest places to visit in Japan. (Chapter 9)

The expat community of Tokyo and Yokohama in the 1950s and 60s used to gather at a group of villas called the "Misaki Houses" perched along the rugged coast of the Miura Peninsula south of Tokyo. These houses later inspired Japan-American fusion architecture. (Chapter 10)

Rocks and caves along the Miura coast. Not all coves are reachable by boat or road. Despite being so close to Tokyo, secret places still remain. (Chapter 10)

Postscript: With regard to clashing signage, Nara's Todaiji Temple was one of the worst offenders (top). And then, in 2019, Todaiji removed it all, restoring the temple to its ancient grandeur (bottom).

For some reason, the kitamae-bune have been largely left out of the history books, at least those which I studied in college. Japanese history as it's usually taught focuses on the big cities near the Pacific coast of Honshu (Osaka, Kyoto, Nagoya and Edo), and the regions around them—with a bit of lip service to the Inland Sea, Kyushu and Shikoku. Living as I do near Kyoto, which has little or no relationship to the sea, the Sea of Japan and the kitamae-bune was a subject that never came up. Only in recent years have I come to realize how important the kitamae-bune were to Japan.

The fact is that Japan is mostly mountainous, and there never was a tradition of building roads or transport by wheeled vehicles. To travel anywhere, you had to walk, sometimes on precipitous mountain paths. The lordly and wealthy might be carried in a palanquin; everyone else went on foot.

As a result, valuable goods were transported by sea and not by land. Although the Pacific side of Japan was more heavily populated, its coasts were exposed and dangerous. Ships hailing from Kyushu or Osaka therefore sailed up the Sea of Japan on the west. It was quicker and safer to transport to a port like Kanazawa and Niigata, and then carry the goods overland for the last stretch of their journey to Edo.

Actually, Edo was only a part of this story. In feudal days, when Japan was less centralized into a few big cities as it is now, there were busy ports and castle towns such as Hagi, Matsue and Kanazawa lining the western coast, making the Sea of Japan route lucrative in its own right. This is why lacquer-making in the town of Wajima on the tip of the Noto Peninsula was able to thrive. Looking at a map of the kitamae-bune ships' courses, you can see that Noto stood right in the middle. Wajima was ideally placed to export its lacquer all over Japan.

We hear much about the Tokaido road, which ran along the Pacific coast from Kyoto to Edo. Its fifty-three stations were immortalized by Hiroshige and other print artists. That's because people walked the Tokaido, and therefore artists took note. Goods went by boat, via the kitamae-bune, up the Sea of Japan. Seaports along the way thrived, but there was no walkable road for most of the journey, and none of the colorful daimyo lordly processions seen on the Tokaido road. The kitamae-bune route didn't lend itself to gold screens and woodblock prints. It went unmemorialized and so today its existence has been largely forgotten.

The kitamae-bune route ran from the port of Osaka, where the great wholesalers had their warehouses, through the Inland Sea via ports such as Tomonoura. At the western edge of the Inland Sea, the boats passed to the Sea of Japan through the straits of Shimonoseki between Honshu and Kyushu. From there the kitamae-bune ships turned northeast and plied their trade along the western coast all the way up to Hokkaido. In the process, dozens of ports grew up including many of the important towns of northern Japan, such as Niigata and Aomori.

Kuroshima was one of these ports. It's one of Japan's larger preserved townscapes, with old houses stretching for many blocks. In

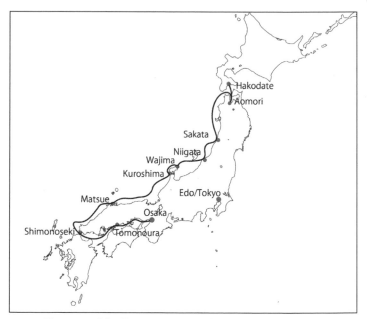

The route of the *kitamae-bune* ships from Osaka to Hokkaido,
via the Inland Sea and up the Sea of Japan coast

The roofs of Kuroshima

contrast to the poor magaki villages, you can feel the prosperity in the black tiled roofs and gray wooden walls fencing off houses from each other. This was a wealthy place.

Of the ten "hidden" regions covered in this book, the Noto Peninsula offered perhaps the widest range of environments. There was the comfortable fishing village of Nakai-minami on the east backed by a hillside lined with temples and shrines. This contrasted with the hardscrabble fishing villages on the windward side, sheltering from harsh winds behind magaki bamboo fences. Inland and on the northern coast we saw well-tended rice paddies, both narrow old-style fields by the coast that hug the lay of the land, and inland, the broad straight-edged new type. To the north is Wajima, Japan's premier lacquer-making center, and down the western coast, is Kuroshima, the prosperous port which was the next one up on the kitamae-bune ships' course north from Kanazawa.

These things co-exist because Noto was formerly far from "hidden." Lying at the heart of the trade routes of western Japan, Noto was where all roads crossed, by land and by sea.

6

Jurassic Beach
Amami Oshima, Kagoshima Prefecture

In 2017 a message showed up on my Facebook page from somebody named Jean-Marc T. The content was that on the island of Amami Oshima, between Kyushu and Okinawa, there was a project to build a massive concrete embankment which would destroy Amami's loveliest beach. Did I have any idea of how we could protect the beach? Along with the message were attached photos of a place called Katoku.

The photos of Katoku's wide bay, with green hills coming down to a shining blue sea, were like a scene from *South Pacific*. At that point I had no idea of what to do, so I simply wrote back, "Hold in there!" But that beautiful image had remained with me.

Then in February 2019, I finally made the trip to Amami in the process of writing this book. On the day before departing, I learned that Jean-Marc and his Amami-born wife, Take Hisami, work as travel guides on the island, so I engaged them to help us. From his name, and the fact that Jean-Marc had communicated with me only in English, I assumed he was a foreigner. I discovered that he's Japanese, with a Japanese mother and French father, educated in Paris. The *T* of "Jean-Marc T" turned out to be his mother's name, Takagi.

Shattered Nio guardian statues

A word on the geography of Amami. As I learned when doing my research for the trip, there's Amami referring to a cluster of islands in the Amami group. And there's the main island of Amami, which is largest. It's rather like "the state of Hawaii," versus the "big island of

Hawaii." Located halfway to Okinawa, the Amami Island group marks the beginning of tropical Japan.

We departed Kyoto with high hopes of seeing Katoku Beach and also Kakeroma, a smaller island just to the south of the main island of Amami. We arrived a bit early at the airport and had some time on our hands before meeting Jean-Marc, so I called him and he recommended that we drive to Amami's northwest peninsula of Imaizaki.

Imaizaki is about thirty minutes from the airport. We drove according to instructions, aiming toward a shrine, Imai Gongen, which stands on a hill near the top of the peninsula. But the roads didn't show up on our map, so we wandered around for quite a while until we finally found it. Obviously rarely visited, the shrine stood at the top of a steep flight of moss-overgrown steps on either side of which were a pair of stone Nio guardian statues that had been shattered and mutilated. Of one, only the legs and feet remained; of the other only the torso. The word *gongen* in the name of the Imai Gongen shrine is a giveaway for Tendai Buddhism, since this was the title used by Tendai for Shinto avatars. We saw this earlier in Toshogu Daigongen, the deified name of first shogun Ieyasu given by Abbot Tenkai of Mount Hiei.

It seemed odd that the *haibutsu kishaku* anti-Buddhist oppression of the early Meiji period would have extended all the way to this distant island. But come to think of it, Amami was ruled at the time by the fief of Satsuma (based in the city of Kagoshima), one of the most radically anti-shogunal fiefs of them all. Back in 1600, the daimyo of Satsuma had been defeated by the first shogun Ieyasu, and his descendants had nurtured the grudge for over two centuries. Finally in 1868 the Satsuma army joined forces with Emperor Meiji to overthrow the shogunate. Saigo Takamori, the charismatic samurai hero of Satsuma had been banished to Amami for a few years in the 1860s, where he had married and fathered several children. After his return to Satsuma, Saigo helped to lead the imperial forces. With such close connections to the fiercest enemies of the shogunate, it's not so strange after all to see scars from the turmoil of the Meiji Restoration.

At the top of the steps stood a small shrine, quietly overlooking the history that unfolded here. Beyond the shrine, up another winding road, we reached a lighthouse with a wide view of the sea. Across Kasari-wan bay, distant mountains floated above twinkling waves. Below us, clinging to the cliffside were thickly growing stretches of sago palms with their wide feathery leaves, and beyond them we could see the curve of the white sand of Imaizaki Beach.

Japan's forests

From the time we had been driving toward Imaizaki, I'd become aware that Amami has relatively few forestry plantations. Most of the natural cover of the land appears to be original forest with the old look of Japan's mountain scenery, soft and fluffy, with many shades of green.

The postwar transformation of Japan's mountains is an unavoidable theme, which crops up in several chapters of this book. It's a subject that you would never see mentioned in a travel book and rarely in any writing on modern Japan. But it colors the experience of anyone traveling or living in the countryside. It's one of Japan's great modern problems—environmental, economic and cultural. It's something that anyone with an interest in Japan's rural landscape needs to know about. So it's time I talked about it in earnest.

Since the late 1940s the mountains of Japan, from Honshu down to Kyushu and Shikoku have been replanted with monoculture plantations of *sugi* cryptomeria and *hinoki* cedar. These evergreens, with their dull uniform foliage make the mountains monotonous and gloomy. It's a completely different landscape from the hills celebrated in old poetry and screen paintings.

Foreign travelers are to be forgiven for not realizing that the forests they're looking at are drastically changed—and all quite recently. Here's a guide to the difference. Sugi and hinoki are evergreens, called in Japanese *shin'yoju*, which means "needle leaf trees." The native forest is overwhelmingly *koyoju* broadleaf deciduous trees. You can see the difference in the color of the forests. The sugi and hinoki are a uniform darkish olive. But the broadleaf forests scintillate with an ever-shifting spectrum of different shades of green.

Native broadleaf forest (Photo by David Caprara)

The broadleaf trees allow light to penetrate to the forest floor, and their fallen leaves fertilize the soil. Within these forests flourishes a riotous jungle of undergrowth, vines and moss. Inside the monoculture plantations, perpetual shadow ensures that nothing except a few ferns will ever grow.

Apart from the color and the fluffiness of the broadleaf forests, another easy way to tell what you're looking at is to see if the trees have grown naturally or stand in nice straight lines. Those striated hillsides with pencil-thin trees growing in rows are planted with sugi and hinoki. Oddly enough, many travelers, including even many Japanese never seem to question whether forests naturally grow this way. They gaze out at a mountainside covered with rows of trees planted in perfect lines and sigh, "Ah, immemorial Japanese nature."

Sugi and hinoki (especially sugi) are favorite government projects so they come with a lot of officially sponsored propaganda. "In 1945 Japan's mountains were denuded after World War II, so that's why we had to start replanting." Not true. In my childhood in the 1960s, and later when I hitchhiked around Japan in 1971, the original forest all

Evergreen plantation (Photo by David Caprara)

around the country was mostly still intact. The big reforestation projects took place after the 1970s, picking up steam in the 1980s—and are continuing now. "Sugi is a hallowed element in traditional wooden construction." Not true. In my work of restoration of old houses, I've seen hundreds of houses across the country, and never once have I come across an old house made of sugi. It just didn't happen.

There's a reason for this, which is that sugi is a low quality wood. It's soft, damages easily and poorly resists damp and insects. The postwar forestation projects favored it simply because it grows fast and straight. Old houses were made with hardier woods such as *tsuga* Japanese hemlock. *Matsu* red pine was favored for flooring, on account of its glossy sheen from its rich supply of sap. While tsuga and matsu are also evergreens, they don't grow as straight as sugi and hinoki, so they weren't favored in the national plantation scheme. Matsu pines were mostly wiped out in a blight after the 1970s, and tsuga is now a semi-endangered tree.

Japan once had towering forests of beautiful broadleaf hardwoods such as *keyaki* zelkova elm, but these have been basically wiped out.

Keyaki grows majestically tall and straight, and its dense beautiful grain qualifies it as "king of Japanese trees." The massive columns of temples such as Myoshinji and Higashi-Honganji in Kyoto are keyaki.

Keyaki has now all but disappeared. Other woods such as *buna* beech and *tochi* horse chestnut (which we saw in Chapter 1 piled up in Tadaura's storehouse of timbers taken from old houses in Ouchi-juku) survive in number only in a few protected reservations and are no longer harvested.

The situation is rich with irony. When it comes to forestry, "Japan, the land of quality" went for low quality. The country lacks good woods to make high-end flooring, walls and furniture. When we restore old houses, we end up importing walnut or elm from America in order to finish them attractively. "Japan, the land of wood," has no good wood!

Which brings us to another myth propagated by the bureaucracies in charge of the reforestation projects: "Sugi and hinoki are necessary for economic growth." The opposite is dramatically true. The value of sugi is so low that the Forestry Agency has built up a truly massive debt. I give talks to groups around Japan about rural revival and often someone comes up to me afterward and says, "We've planted our land with sugi, but now it's almost worthless. It costs more to cut down the sugi than they're worth. What to do?"

More about sugi cedar

Tree plantation is not inherently a bad thing. The mistake has been monoculture with fast-growing, low quality evergreens. One can imagine a scenario in which, for example, the government had planted deciduous forests of keyaki elm which grow tall and straight, while at the same time producing a wood that is finer even than the best American elm. One keyaki log seventy years old would be worth easily two hundred sugi. The international demand for fine woods is ever growing, so Japan would now have a thriving export business of high-quality wood, instead of importing high-grade lumber.

So far I've spoken of the economic mess of sugi, but there's also an environmental disaster. Wild animals can't live in the sugi death forest, so they descend into the villages where they wreak havoc with farmers' crops. The shallow roots of the sugi allow for fast erosion, which fills the streams with silt, which leads to more building of dams and riverside erosion walls. Sugi and hinoki grow tall and thin, and are pruned to have few or no lower branches. So when a typhoon or heavy rains come, the trees tip over en masse, and with their shallow roots the plantations are prone to landslides.

Finally we have the sugi pollen which afflicts tens of millions of Japanese with severe allergies every spring. In the spring you can see great clouds of pollen rising from the hills. For many this triggers lifelong allergic illnesses, and in fact Japan's population now suffers from some of the highest allergy afflictions in the world. The cost of treating these allergies alone wipes out any economic benefit that the sugi might bring.

Of course, sugi and hinoki did exist in Japan's native forest. In old paintings you see rolling hillsides of deciduous forest, with the odd sugi or hinoki sticking up here and there. Sugi were something of a rarity, making these trees rather special. This, plus the fact that they are among Japan's longest-living trees, and can grow to towering heights, caused them to be favored by Shinto as sacred trees. You often find them standing in the grounds of shrines. Lord Matsudaira Masatsuna in the early 1600s spent twenty years planting sugi along the approaches to Toshogu Shrine in Nikko. It was his way to pay respects with this very special tree to the first Tokugawa shoguns who were enshrined there. Four hundred years later, these stately trees are now one of the treasures of Nikko.

Some of my favorite ancient trees in Japan are sugi. A few of the oldest are in Iya Valley and nearby villages of central Shikoku. The island of Yakushima, between Amami and Kyushu, is especially famous for its sugi which are more than a thousand years old. These old sugi appear so different from the trees on the plantations as to almost look like a different species.

As can be seen in Iya or in Yakushima, sugi trees, left to nature,

A six-hundred-year-old *sugi* cedar at Gosho Shrine, Iya Valley, Shikoku

don't grow tall and straight, like American redwoods. Instead the really old sugi have relatively short but massive trunks from which huge branches sprout at odd angles. The heavy thickness, combined with the rugged curving branches that seem like the limbs and tails of dinosaurs, make these trees into powerful living beings with monstrous and mysterious power. That's what sugi originally were.

The problem is not sugi per se. It's an important tree for Japan, a sacred tree for shrines. But with the postwar plantations, sugi outgrew its natural balance. From being a benign local tree, it became a damaging invasive species. At this point about 40 percent of Japan's total forest land has been covered with sugi and hinoki. Hokkaido, perhaps because it's so far north, has fewer plantations. Remove Hokkaido from the calculation, and the figure of 40 percent likely rises to over 60 percent for the rest of the country. Despite the environmental, economic and cultural disaster that is sugi, the government, once set on its ways, cannot turn back. So the project continues despite nobody having any idea what to do with all this unsellable and unusable sugi.

As for what the forests look like, the replanting has been done in patchwork fashion. It's not as if there are wide expanses of native forest, and then big areas of plantations. It wasn't carried out according to a master plan, but simply according to who accepted the government subsidies for planting first. Some landowners planted early on, others later or never. It's all mixed up, so when you look at typical mountain scenery, you'll see a patch of plantation over here, then some native trees and then another strip of plantation over there and so on. Finding an unimpaired native forest is difficult, because there's bound to be a patch cut out and planted with sugi or hinoki somewhere. You see this vividly in the autumn, when the patchwork reveals itself as a sea of olive green interspersed with occasional strips of red and yellow.

This discussion of plantations and sugi comes, rather incongruously, in the chapter about Amami, where the mountains struck me as beautiful precisely because they had so few sugi. This brings me to one of the big themes of this book, which is, a lot of what I was searching for as I traveled through "Hidden Japan" was *things that are not there*. That is, rural villages without aluminum railings, tin huts and blue plastic sheeting; oceanside cliffs without concrete embankments; temples and shrines without garish signage; and mountains without sugi and hinoki.

Despite being known as the land of aesthetics, the physical environment of Japan could be better called the land of junk. It's overwhelming, all-enveloping. Tourists, Japanese and foreign, simply don't see it because they're so focused on finding what's beautiful. That's a credit to their love of Japan. But the junk is there nonetheless.

Thinking back to the writer Shirasu Masako and our first meeting in 1994, the subject of our discussion was "what's real." It's still my subject. I'm as eager to find the beautiful and wonderful in this country as any devoted Japan-lover, but I can't overlook the junk. Because it's all too "real." So, when we find a scenic village of just rice paddies and some old houses—with nothing else; cliffs and seashore not scarred by public works; shrines and temples uncluttered with bright red warnings and advertisements; and best of all, brilliant green hillsides that breathe the lush jungly air of Japan's original forests—these are discoveries beyond price.

It's a kind of fluke that the cold dark hand of Japanese modern forestry has so far been withheld (mostly) from Amami. Seeing these hills brought back to me the old joy I used to have in traveling in Japan's countryside.

Mangroves

Later we met up with Jean-Marc and Hisami and headed down toward Katoku, stopping along the way to see the mangrove swamps which are one of the premier tourist draws of Amami. In these days of over-tourism, I find that "tourist draws" are usually disappointing and try to avoid them. But—maybe it was due to the slight rain that was falling—that day there were very few people there and we could see the mangroves at leisure. They spread over a far wider area than I was expecting. With the mist rising over them in the distance, they looked like a primeval fantasy.

From the mangroves we drove further south, through mountains where they're building a new Self-Defense Forces base, with the usual gashed hillsides and concrete walls typical of Japanese civil engineering. So far the damage to Amami's environment has been contained, but one wonders what future years of such construction will bring. One can't be too optimistic.

Construction in Amami

Endangered Katoku Beach

We followed the course of a small river, which when it reached the coast swelled into a wide inlet. At the time we arrived the wind had dropped and the still surface of the water reflected the cliffs on the other side like a mirror. We walked through a small hamlet consisting of a handful of houses set back from the bay and took a path down to the seaside, where the view opened up to the magical vista I had seen in Jean-Marc's photos, like a flawless beach on a South Pacific island. A hardy seaside plant named *adan* (pandanus) with long spiky leaves had been planted at the side of the dunes, which helped to protect the sand from erosion and the hamlet from winds and high waves. Beyond and above it all rose jungly mountains in rich green.

The people of Amami call Katoku "Jurassic Beach." Standing there with bated breath I thought to myself, "Incredible—a pristine beach like this still exists!"

But in the "construction state," preserving such a place is not easy. That's the tragic reality of modern Japan. There's a plan to build a massive 21-foot (6.5-meter)-tall concrete embankment stretching the length of the beach. It's for the announced purpose of protecting the beach from erosion, but in recent years, even in typhoon years, there's been no erosion.

As in the case of many other civil engineering works, officials mandate the concrete primarily to use up budgets so contractors and bureaucrats can profit. They are not responding to a real need. Yet, the work must go on. The day after our arrival we learned that construction was about to begin. Jean-Marc and other Amami citizens who have joined to try to protect the beach have gained support from a group of lawyers who are fighting the construction plans. Despite their efforts, once the building work has actually started, there's close to no hope of stopping it. Very soon, Jurassic Beach will disappear from Japan.

It's a desperate situation, but the people who love Katoku are keeping up their struggle. The case of the old harbor of Tomonoura in the Inland Sea gives cause for hope. Tomonoura, Japan's last remaining

Edo-period seaport, was also threatened with a destructive landfill project, but after decades of lawsuits the locals finally won their case, and in 2016 the landfill was stopped. So miracles do happen.

This brings me to another of the main themes of this book. All over Japan, in mountain villages and on small islands, beautiful scenery still survives, "holy sites" worthy of pilgrimage. But these are fragile, threatened. Forever-expanding public works and lack of interest in natural and cultural heritage on the part of a majority of citizens mean that for most of these places, their days are numbered. In two of my previous books, *Dogs and Demons* (2001) and *Theory of Japanese Landscape* (2014, in Japanese only), I probed the mechanisms that feed the degradation of countryside and old towns. Sadly, those processes continue at an increasing pace.

Maybe it's Japan's predestined fate for its beautiful places to be debased. If not encased in concrete, they are reduced to one protected spot amidst a sea of visual pollution. When you visit a lovely village you have to ask yourself whether if you came back in a year's time, or ten years' time, the same beauty would still be there. With a pang, you realize that no, it won't be. In the future, many of the locations I've written about in this book will be greatly altered, the qualities that made them magical lost.

Shirasu Masako said, "Introducing hidden hamlets to the world is a crime." I have the same fear, but at the same time, I feel I need to tell people about these precious survivals, while appealing to my readers: "Wondrous things still exist. Let's value them and look after them."

For me, as well as for the group working to save Katoku, all we can do is continue, more or less blindly. The struggle for those on the ground such as Jean-Marc and his friends is a hard one, but it's the duty of people who love these places. We only can pray that another miracle will occur.

An avenue of ancient trees

From Katoku Beach, Jean-Marc and Hisami guided us on a visit to Kakeroma Island, located just south of the main island of Amami. To get there you take a ferry from the port of Koniya in Setouchi town on the southern coast of Amami. It's only a twenty-minute ride, but in order to save money on the ferry cost, we left our car at Koniya, and used the car that Jean-Marc and Hisami keep on Kakeroma, where they have a second house in the hamlet of Shodon.

Kakeroma is a small island, but its zigzag salamander-like shape branches into numerous small bays and peninsulas. Shodon, near to the ferry dock, is a hamlet similar to those in Okinawa with houses enclosed by stone walls made of rough volcanic or coral rocks. Through those houses run narrow lanes, quiet, nearly devoid of people.

Growing beside the doorway to Jean-Marc and Hisami's house was an *ako* tree (*ficus superba*), a rare semitropical tree with wide twisting branches. I had seen an ako tree once before, a grand ancient one spreading almost as wide as a city block, on the island of Ojika in the Goto archipelago off the west coast of Nagasaki Prefecture, where I did a house restoration project.

The seeds of the ako tree, looking like small berries, fruit not amidst twigs and leaves, but on the trunk and thick branches of the tree itself. This was a meeting with an old friend. But it was just the beginning of our meeting with trees on Kakeroma Island.

From Jean-Marc and Hisami's house it was a two-minute walk to the beach where a curving embankment was lined with a row of ancient *deigo* trees. Known commonly as Tiger's Claw in English, these are found in Africa and India, across the southern Pacific and in Okinawa. Like the ako, their roots spread wide at the base, while the branches twist and turn like those in a fairy-tale forest.

The deigo trees here have especially thick trunks, and the interlocking branches wormed and wriggled their way thickly over our heads. I've seen other roadside tree plantings in Japan, but none this beautiful. Even in Europe this view would be considered exceptional. I heard that these trees are hundreds of years old. The deigo-lined walkway at Shodon had the feel of something mythic, a scene from prehistory or legend.

In Japan today, a stand of trees with wide branches stretching out in their natural condition is a rare sight. As mentioned earlier, "fallen leaves are dirty," "tree branches are inconvenient"—this attitude has sunk deep into modern Japanese culture. Everywhere, extending branches are lopped off.

A few years ago, I visited the city of Maebashi in Gunma Prefecture north of Tokyo, and was struck by a double row of tall keyaki elm trees lining the street in front of the railway station. The long branches soared up and up, creating the distinctive "gothic arch" of high elms, sleek and stately. It was autumn and the yellow and wine red of the changing leaves shone as the afternoon light slanted through the branches. When I met the mayor I commented, "Your keyaki avenue is a true treasure." He responded, "We also love these trees. But there are many among the town's citizens who don't. We're bombarded with constant complaints, 'we hate falling leaves,' 'too much shade,' and so forth. We might have to cut them all down."

Aside from the "dirty" falling leaves, there's an even stronger argument against old trees which is that they are "dangerous." To a surprising degree, this has become an orthodoxy in modern Japan. A friend told me about a roadside stand of old cherry trees near where he lives in Yokohama which the city cut down to the base, for the reason that, being seventy years old, they had become dangerous. There's a term that has recently become prevalent in Japanese city planning: "preemptive cutting." Long before there's even one rotten branch, the tree gets chopped down as a preemptive measure.

When it comes to trees, "tall" and "old" no longer mean, as they once did in Japan, awe-inspiring and divine. They mean a threat to the public's well-being, and one by one (or in the case of Meiji Gaien park in Tokyo, a thousand at one stroke) you can see these being removed, from private gardens, city parks, university campuses, shrine and temple grounds and even mountain paths.

With this background, one can imagine how precious is this row of deigo trees. They run counter to modern Japan. One can't help but imagine the danger they stand in.

The deigo trees as they stand now are still strong and healthy. I say to myself with a sigh, "The time may come soon when these will be destroyed." Perhaps it was because we came here right after Jurassic Beach, which indeed will be destroyed, that I was hypersensitive and my imagination ran away with me.

Banyans and a beach

It was hard to tear ourselves away from the otherworldly scenery of the deigo trees, but we set out driving toward Saneku Beach near the western edge of Kakeroma Island. Along the way, Hisami said, "There's something I want to show you," so we made a detour at a small hamlet called Takena.

Takena also had a sandy beach, but we turned away from it, walking inland on a small path. Soon we reached deep forest, and suddenly I found myself facing a breathtaking huge *gajumaru* tree.

Gajumaru (*ficus microcarpa*) is a kind of banyan tree, which I had seen on the island of Yaeyama in Okinawa, but this one was several times larger. As I was looking at it, Hisami called, "Take a few more steps further into forest." When I did, I saw that at the spot that Hisami was pointing to was a truly massive gajumaru, steeped in spirit

A giant *gajumaru* tree

Idyllic Saneku Beach

power. To my embarrassment, so enraptured has I been with the first tree, that I had completely overlooked the true giant just beyond it.

Like the banyan trees one sees in Southeast Asia, the branches spread wide against the sky, and from them they dropped narrow roots, which once they reached the ground became stems and trunks for further extensions of the tree. Old growth wild banyans grow with such complexity that one can hardly tell what's a branch, a trunk or a root. We heard that this tree is said to be over one thousand years old. You could feel nature breathing.

Driving further, we neared Saneku Beach near the western tip of the island. After viewing it from a distance from a hill as we approached, we parked at the beach and walked along the sands as the setting sun lit up the sea and surrounding hills.

From a distance the beach looked flawlessly beautiful, but once arrived we saw it was littered by uncountable pieces of plastic and metal debris. This is not to be blamed on Amami locals or visitors. It arrives from across the seas, from the other islands of Japan, as well as from China and Korea. Not to mention garbage jettisoned by passing ships.

This is hardly unique to Amami and is a problem faced by islands and beaches across the globe. But on the islands of Amami, which are in much more pristine shape than most of Japan, one wonders, "Is there nothing that could be done about this?"

For the construction that will destroy Katoku, I have no idea how much is involved, but it will cost at least several million dollars of tax money. Rural towns addicted to public construction largesse dream up project after project, leading them into a cycle of over-construction. Suppose one took the annual construction funding and set some of it aside to support a "Seaside Cleaning Crew." The people working on cleaning the beaches would have an income at least as good as they presently enjoy from road and embankment building. Wasteful public works projects would decrease and the beaches would be cleaned up. And to the bureaucrats' pleasure, the town and prefecture would have the same amount of money to play with in their budgets. Three birds with one stone.

Aside from beach cleaning, one can think of other ways to profitably spend the construction money. For example, at Katoku Beach or Shodon hamlet, where there are plenty of *akiya* abandoned houses in the distinctive Amami-Okinawa southern style, you could fix up some as guesthouses and these would bring in income. With some creative planning, one can think of ways to leave Amami much like it is, but in better shape to meet the future. Well, I know all this is daydreaming.

On the way back from Saneku Beach, I noticed that the trees along the cliffsides facing the sea had slim silvery trunks which reminded me of the koa trees from my Hawaii childhood. Still lost in memory, I found that our car had reached Yuhi-no-oka "Sunset Hill," a viewing point from which we could look out over the gulf between Kakeroma and the main Amami Island. The sun was sinking beyond the horizon and the sky was dyed red.

Sunset view

The view over the Oshima Strait was calm and dreamlike. Across the gulf on the Amami side we could see the small western port of Nishi-komi, a part of Setouchi township. When we visited in March 2019 it was due to be redeveloped. An American cruise company proposed a plan for huge cruise ships from China to visit Amami, with the port facilities to be built at Nishikomi. Once the port expansion began, it would involve the construction of access roads, seaside embankments, shopping centers and more, ultimately affecting the entire western half of the gulf. The scenery would be drastically transformed.

Advanced under the name of tourist promotion, large scale cruise operations would seem to be the ultimately lucrative venture. However when you get thousands of people descending all at once on a small island or beach it can literally destroy the place. Plus, the income isn't what it seems to be. In Southeast Asia, they call tourism of this type "zero-dollar tourism." When the passengers alight, they don't go to the local shops; they buy at a visitor center at outlets owned by the cruise line or their investors. Because they eat and sleep on board the ship, not much profit accrues to the locals. Meanwhile the island's scenery and environment receives devastating damage.

The view from Yuhi-no-oka was one threatened soon with destruction. But fortunately the citizens of Setouchi rose up in opposition and in August 2019 the town announced that the plan was canceled. Ordinarily, no matter how much the public objects to them, public works projects such as this are usually unstoppable. In modern Japan, what happened at Setouchi is truly exceptional. Thanks to the township's decision, the southern part of Amami is spared.

Or is it? In *Dogs and Demons*, I had pointed out that these projects are like the robot from the future in the movie *Terminator*. Indestructible, you can slice off an arm, crush its legs, it will still come after you. In the case of the old port of Tomonoura in Hiroshima Prefecture, after decades of struggle led by local citizens, they finally won a conclusive victory at court and the landfill was stopped. But that hasn't been the end of it. Afterward, under the new name of "seashore protection," plans to pour concrete around the harbor still proceed. In the case of Amami, Nishikomi was saved this time, but who knows when a similar plan will be proposed again. One really can't relax. And so with an unsettled heart, we watched the sun set over the Oshima Strait.

Japan's Gaugin

Amami's natural surroundings strike at something deep in the soul. In the years after World War II, an artist named Tanaka Isson, attracted by Amami's strange appeal, moved here from Chiba Prefecture near Tokyo. During his lifetime he was poor and went nearly completely unnoticed by the art world. But in recent years he's been rediscovered and is now called "Japan's Gauguin." People have felt that his move to Amami was like Gauguin's move to Tahiti.

Near the airport there's a small but well-outfitted museum where one can view Isson's works. When you see them in real life, they feel less like Gauguin and more like the French primitivists. Where Gauguin focused on people, Isson took nature itself as his subject. Isson painted ferns, adan pandanus, gajumaru trees and tropical birds in the naïve and dreamlike style of a jungle by primitivist artist Rousseau.

Joy and fear

At Amami I found the natural environment surviving in better shape than any other place I've visited in Japan. Its islands are covered still with mostly natural forests, and lovely beaches spared by big leisure developments remain in good condition. We came across truly magical scenes like the deigo trees at Shodon.

On the other hand, Katoku Beach is likely doomed. According to the latest word from Jean-Marc, in early 2023 preparations for pouring the concrete for the embankment were proceeding. If a miracle doesn't happen, Jurassic Beach will be wiped out. The deigo trees at Shodon are fine right now, but one worries about their future.

To travel around "Hidden Japan" is to discover wonders that pull at the heartstrings, and at the same time to grieve over the grim future facing these things. There's an undercurrent of terror at the near-irresistible advance of the degradation. I suppose the terror is part of the thrill of travel in Japan.

Susa Hornfels

Sea of Japan

Shimane
Prefecture

Hagi Castle
Tokoji

Higashi-
Ushirobata

Hagi

Sasanami-ichi

Akiyoshidai

Yamaguchi

Yamaguchi
Prefecture

Rurikoji
Joeiji

Inland Sea

7
Old Castle Town
Hagi, Yamaguchi Prefecture

M any of the "hidden places" of today were far from hidden in earlier eras, when they were thriving cultural centers. With this in mind, my traveling companions and I thought to explore one of the old regional cities of Japan that in former days had been capitals of their own little kingdoms. We settled on Hagi in Yamaguchi Prefecture.

When you look back at the Edo period, feudalism is the defining feature. In Kyoto lived the emperor and the court nobles; in Edo was the shogun. The rest of Japan was ruled over by three hundred daimyo lords, and in each of their domains the culture differed. Until the Meiji Restoration, Japan was not so much one country as a conglomeration of three hundred city states, like Italy in the nineteenth century.

The largest castle towns, Edo, Osaka, Nagoya and Kanazawa, remain as populous cities today, but after Japan opened up to the West in the 1870s after centuries of isolation, they were greatly modernized. While some castles and bits of old neighborhoods are still there to be seen, one doesn't feel much the weight of history.

Hagi was once one of the greatest regional towns, but for better or for ill, after the Meiji period, it fell out of Japan's mainstream, failed to be developed and so never grew into a big modern city. While known as a tourist destination, Hagi no longer features on history's main stage. In this town, perhaps, we could discover traces of the local culture of the Edo era.

With that expectation, we boarded the bullet train from Kyoto. At

Shin-Yamaguchi Station, we changed to a rental car, but drove first not to Hagi but to two temples we wanted to see in Yamaguchi City, Rurikoji and Joeiji.

What's now the prefecture of Yamaguchi consisted of two old domains, Nagato-no-kuni, which comprised Hagi and the west coast and Suo-no-kuni which spread over the east and south. After 1600, these were unified as Choshu Fief, with its main capital at Hagi and a secondary capital at Yamaguchi. In the last years of the Edo period, they moved the main capital to Yamaguchi.

During Edo, the ruling family of Choshu was the Mori clan, but up until the great battle of Sekigahara in 1600, the Ouchi clan had ruled here for centuries. The town of Yamaguchi had a similar terrain to Kyoto, so the Ouchi rulers drew up a Kyoto-like grid-like city plan, and in the fourteenth and fifteenth century built here the "Western Capital."

After the devastating Onin War of 1467–77, Japan was thrown into chaos for well over a century, and during that time many court nobles and artists such as the great genius of ink painting, Sesshu, fled here. During those years Yamaguchi flourished, while Kyoto, riven by civil war, was repeatedly burned to the ground.

In the sixteenth century, the Ouchi clan declined and ultimately vanished. By the end of the century the civil wars finally reached Yamaguchi, with the result that it too was burned down, and little remains of that era within the city center. But traces can be found sprinkled in the hills around town.

At Rurikoji, located at the edge of town, stands a five-story pagoda dating from 1442 in which we could sense something of the glory of the old Western Capital. Of Japan's surviving five-story pagodas, this is the tenth oldest. From the point of view of age, Nara's Horyuji (seventh century), Muroji (eighth or ninth century) and Kyoto's Daigoji (tenth century), are much older. But none of the others can compete for sheer elegance.

The roofs are thatched with *hiwada-buki* cedar bark, not tiles, which brings—as we saw at the shrine buildings of Hiyoshi Shrine

The five-story pagoda of Rurikoji Temple

(Momoyama period) and the *tahoto* pagoda at Ishiyama-dera Temple (Kamakura period)—a particular gentleness to the rooflines, exuding a sense of refinement.

The width of each floor of this pagoda tapers slightly as it rises, lending it a graceful slimness. The step-by-step rise of the upward-turning eaves creates a gentle feeling of movement, like a leisurely jellyfish pulsing upward.

Horyuji's ancient five-story pagoda—Japan's oldest—is very much in muscular "Chinese style" with tiled roofs, and so it creates a rather strong and hard-edged impression. Muroji's small pagoda, done with hiwada-buki, charms with its cuteness. But here, Rurikoji's pagoda, with its lines like the wings of a bird, and impressive overall scale, succeeds better than all the rest in producing the effect of *miyabi*, the courtly elegance of old Kyoto.

Such a thing is long lost from Kyoto itself. You need to go into the countryside to find the miyabi that once dwelled in Kyoto.

Since ancient times many pagodas have been built across Japan, but most of them have disappeared, and for that reason the ones that remain are truly precious. Rurikoji is one of the finest of them all.

A sixteenth-century and a twentieth-century garden

To the northeast of Rurikoji stands the temple of Joeiji. This too is a relic of the Ouchi's "Western Capital." Celebrated fifteenth-century monk-artist Sesshu took refuge with the Ouchis and designed a garden here.

Sesshu is a magic name in Japanese art history. He's known as the Saint of Painting, for his highly abstract ink paintings. A monk associated with Kyoto's Zen temples, he traveled to China and brought back with him Ming painting techniques. Among them was the art of *haboku* "splashed ink," in which, with a whisk of the brush here, a splash and a dot there, the painter marvelously conjures towering peaks and valleys.

Sesshu was also a garden designer, which was a natural development because gardens were seen as three-dimensional ink paintings. You can find many gardens around Japan supposedly designed by Sesshu. In Yamaguchi and Shimane prefectures alone there are at least five or six locations, although it's unclear what claim any of them have to be genuine. Among the "attributed to Sesshu" gardens, the one at Joeiji Temple stands out for its expansive and dynamic design.

The garden uses the technique of "standing stones," with squarish sharp-edged rocks placed in great abundance. The rough power is eye-catching. Standing stones, with jagged rocks placed upright, is a

The Sesshu garden, Joeiji Temple

mark of fifteenth- and sixteenth-century gardens, and we see it vividly here. Garden designers of this era aimed to replicate the mood of a painted ink landscape. They replaced the two dimensions of ink and paper with the three dimensions of sand, grass, moss, water and stone. Their gardens were expanded paintings, designed to be seen from a particular angle, like gazing at a hanging scroll. In this case, the viewpoint is the temple verandah. Seen from this vantage point, a jumble of pointed rocks spreads out over a grassy space in the foreground; at the back of the garden there is a rise to the right, where a cascade of rocks suggests a distant waterfall.

With the standing stones like craggy mountain peaks and the flow from the waterfall, the garden imparts the mood of a landscape painting. One can imagine that this really is by Sesshu. Afterward, looking at paintings by Sesshu, I noticed that his mountains looked rather like the rocks in this garden.

The Sesshu garden spreads out on the inner side of the temple. On the front side, near the entry gate is a modern garden, Nanmeitei, one of the last works by the twentieth-century garden designer Shigemori Mirei. It's supposed to represent the sea voyage of Sesshu when he went to study in Ming China. The white sand is the sea and the angular standing stones are very prominent.

I've seen similar standing stones in other gardens designed by Mirei, and after coming here, I get the feeling that he acquired the Muromachi-era style and feel from Joeiji's Sesshu garden. In contrast to Sesshu's wildness, Mirei's garden is highly "designed." White gravel and moss have become major design motifs and make at least as strong an impression as the stones themselves. It's an instructive contrast to see, on either side of the main hall of Joeiji, two gardens separated by four hundred years.

A small market town

From Joeiji we drove toward Hagi along the Sea of Japan coast. On the way we passed the small town of Sasanami-ichi, which has been designated by the national government as a *Judenken* "historical collection of old houses." The town is marked by houses tiled with ocher-colored *sekishu-gawara* roof tiles.

Our main aim for this visit was to tour the town of Hagi, but Hagi is rather special in that it was the seat of the lord's castle and a hub for merchants and craftsmen. However, in feudal fiefs of the Edo period, the majority of people lived in the countryside. They were farmers, fishermen or foresters and it's in their small villages where the old culture of Edo can be seen most vividly. In those days not only the look of villages but even fields and forests varied from domain to domain, taking many different forms. Whether it's the shape of the houses, the color of roof tiles, the way streets are laid out or the design of temples and shrines, each had its own local style.

The ocher sekishu-gawara roof tiles, made in Shimane Prefecture, are one of those distinctively local things that tell you you're not in Kyoto anymore. Japanese roof tiles tend to be black or gray. But from Okayama through Hiroshima prefectures and on to the Sea of Japan, you see reddish roofs reminiscent of the Mediterranean.

In small towns that were far from Kyoto and Edo, population density was low compared to the capital cities, so they suffered less when earthquakes came. They were less likely to be caught up in great wars, and so escaped many of the battles and fires, with the result that much that was lost at the center remains quietly in these villages. Rurikoji's pagoda, Joeiji's garden and the village of Sasanami-ichi are such places.

I love towns like Sasanami-ichi and was greatly tempted to explore it. I was intrigued to see what unusual elements might be found in a village of conservative Choshu Fief. But I satisfied myself with taking photos from the highway above it so we could get to Hagi in time. Saved for the next visit.

The rise and fall of the Obaku Zen sect

From Sasanami-ichi it was about thirty minutes to Hagi. Before entering Hagi proper, we paid a visit to Tokoji Temple to the northeast of town. In this temple's grounds are to be found the graves of the Mori clan who ruled Hagi during the Edo period.

I took one look at the *somon* entry gate and realized this must be an Obaku Zen temple. Painted cinnabar red, it consisted of two lower wings with a higher central section surmounted by finlike roof flares in shape of a mythical *makara* sea monster. The form of this gate was similar to the *pailou* ceremonial gates one sees in Chinatowns. All of these are marks of the Obaku sect of Zen whose head temple, Mampukuji, is in Uji south of Kyoto.

To pause for a moment to talk about Obaku, it was the only new religion ever officially recognized by the shogunate during the Edo period. In the 1640s, during the early years of Edo, the Ming Empire collapsed and the charismatic Zen monk Ingen fled from China to Japan. Invited to Edo, Ingen had an audience with the fourth shogun, seventeen-year-old Tokugawa Ietsuna, whom he hugely impressed. Ietsuna supported Ingen and granted him land in Uji to build Mampukuji Temple.

Following this, for a full century until the later 1700s, the abbots of Mampukuji were all monks who came from China. They brought with them Zen rituals, as well as Ming architecture, calligraphy and music, which went on to influence everything from temple chants to the drums and flutes of summer Obon festival dances. Compared to the two other large Zen sects (Soto and Rinzai) which had become very well-behaved and Japanese, Obaku's fresh Chinese ways of thought were invigorating. For this reason, and because the muscle of the shogunate was behind it, daimyo lords across the land built Obaku temples as their ancestral temples. It became the fashion to enshrine the graves of the lord's family within an Obaku temple.

One wonders if the Obaku abbots also brought with them the Chinese approach to ancestral tombs, such as the Ming Tombs, whose avenues are lined with stone sculptures. This grand approach to noble tombs may account for why feudal lords chose Obaku temples as the preferred sites for their graves.

For example, the temple of Zuiryuji in Toyama was built by the lord of Kaga Fief in 1614 as his family's ancestral temple. It's now a Soto Zen temple, but Obaku influence is all over it. The axial temple layout is pure Obaku, and around the precincts you see plaques written by Ingen and his disciples. Between Zuiryuji and the lord's grave, in the grand "Ming tombs" tradition, is a row of stone lanterns nearly eight city blocks long. A stone megalith as high as a three-story building towers over the graveyard. Obaku ancestral temples did not do things in half measures.

With the advent of the Meiji Restoration, the Obaku Zen sect suffered great damage. It symbolized the old power structure of the shogun and daimyo lords, so hundreds of Obaku temples across Japan were destroyed in the *haibutsu kishaku* anti-Buddhist movement of the 1870s. With that background, I was pleased to see that Tokoji has survived as an Obaku temple.

A philosopher's walk

From a gate you can learn much about the temple inside. The shape of the somon entry gate was enough to tell me that this is an Obaku temple. In fact, gates are such a major feature of Japanese temples that in my book *Another Kyoto*, I devoted the first chapter just to them. You go to see a famous temple, but when you arrive, you see no temple, just a gate. Pass through that, and there's another gate. Only much further in do you arrive at the temple itself. Sometimes the gates are as grand or even more beautiful than the temple they lead to.

This progression of gates has to do with the idea of leaving the mundane world behind, and progressing up higher spiritual levels, stage by stage, gate by gate. The avenue leading under the gates is the *sando*, the central axis. It represents the sacred mountain around which the universe revolves. In fact, the word used for most temples' main gate, *sanmon*, literally means "mountain gate," reminding us that we're climbing up toward a sacred peak. One could think of the series of gates as base camps along the way. Some temples, especially Obaku-style Zen temples have an especially imposing sando.

This is true of Tokoji. The temple grounds are perfectly axial, centered on one long sando walkway. After the somon gate, you walk for a while until you reach the imposing sanmon. This is the true main gate

The pine-tree-lined *sando* walkway at Tokoji Temple

to the complex. The small outer somon was just a decorative prelude. Beyond the sanmon, at the far end of the path, framed by pine trees, you glimpse the Daiyuhoden main hall.

When Ingen and his disciples arrived, bringing Ming-style writing and brushwork with them, they created a sensation in the world of Japanese calligraphy. Ever since then, people have looked to Obaku as a calligraphy treasure house. Therefore when visiting an Obaku temple, it pays to look carefully at the plaques above gates and doors. Above the sanmon gate at Tokoji is a plaque by the famed monk Sokuhi, known as one of the "Three Calligraphers of Obaku," that reads Gedatsu-mon "Gate of Liberation." Its quirky Zen brushstrokes tell you that in passing through this gate you have left your old life behind. Later, at the Daiyuhoden Hall, I saw plaques by Ingen and his chief disciple Mokuan who became the Second Abbot of Mampukuji. Each of these plaques, like the gates, marks a step in spiritual progress.

It isn't something that foreign visitors can easily do, but it's an added plus if someone along with you can manage to read the inscriptions on the calligraphic plaques. Especially in Obaku Zen temples, there

The graveyard of the Mori clan, Tokoji Temple

are always words with an eccentric and thought-provoking twist. In general, temples consist of far more than the central worship hall itself; there are the gates, calligraphic plaques, weatherworn stones and ancient trees along the way. As Keats wrote, "the trees / That whisper round a temple become soon / Dear as the temple's self."

Part of the attraction of Obaku temples lies in the old pine trees planted in the grounds. Pine trees are typical of Zen in general, and at Obaku they refer back to the pine groves of Confucius' hometown of Qufu. Confucius and his disciples would walk in the pine groves talking of philosophy. The pine-lined sando path of an Obaku temple is a "philosopher's walk."

In the old days, Zuiryuji Temple in Toyama also had a path lined with ancient pines and *keyaki* elms, but when the government restored it from 1985–1995, they cut the trees down and covered the courtyards with stretches of grass and white gravel. It was done so that the public could have a clear view of the newly restored temple buildings, and also to fit in with a modern idea of Zen minimalism. The view of Zuiryuji's magnificent temples is there. But the pines that shaded the philosophers are gone. Luckily at Tokoji, the pines still stand densely, and one can walk amongst them sunk in thought.

Graveyards as power spots

As we walked onward, we found behind the Daiyuhoden Hall an area dedicated to the Choshu samurai who fought in the struggle against the shogunate in the last years of the Edo period, with gravestones for the "Four Heroes and Eleven Martyrs." Beyond this, past a little gate, we found an astonishing sight.

It was a truly grand graveyard, done in the same vein as the row of stone lanterns and colossal monolith at Zuiryuji. The sando walkway was divided into three stone paths laid out in a field of gravel, and extending into the distance in geometrical lines were five hundred stone lanterns on a slight incline. Those were dedicated to family retainers. At the top were five *torii* gates, and behind them on a raised platform, ten stone monuments to the Mori lords of Choshu and their consorts. To the left and right of this tableau were smaller grave areas with similar arrangements of twenty stone torii, but lower, accompanied by stone markers for family members and concubines.

The combination of torii gates with Buddhist-style gravestones is extremely unusual. The date of the building of this graveyard is not marked anywhere, but judging by the geometric layout, I suppose that it was built in late Edo or the early years of Meiji. The torii are likely a relic of the era, when the government was establishing *Kokka Shinto* "National Shinto." Of course, in a much earlier era when Shinto and Buddhism were still unified, you could also sometimes see this arrangement. For example, at Nikko, beyond the high torii gates and shrine halls, at the highest level is a Buddhist-style bronze monument containing the bones of shogun Tokugawa Ieyasu.

As grand as are the sando walkway and tombstones of the Mori clan and its retainers at Tokoji, it's not the only graveyard of the Moris. In fact there are four locations in Yamaguchi Prefecture.

Tokoji commemorates odd-numbered lords from the third lord to the eleventh lord. There's another temple to the southwest of Hagi called Daishoin, which commemorates the first lord Hidenari, and all the even-numbered lords from the second lord to the twelfth lord. Inside the castle town of Hagi is yet another graveyard, Tenjuin-seki, with a monument to Terumoto, the father of the first lord. The tombs of the thirteenth and fourteenth lords and their children are situated in the grounds of Rurikoji Temple which we saw at the start of our trip. These were built after the Choshu lords moved their capital to Yamaguchi at the end of Edo, and they're suitably imposing.

Graveyards are natural power spots. They're also "meditation spots" that lead us to ruminate about the brevity of life. Not limited to Japan of course, graveyards everywhere provide this rich human experience, for example, the Jewish Cemetery of Prague, where the tombstones lie scattered, fallen over and half-buried in the soil.

At the temple settlement on Mount Koya, south of Nara, the center of the Shingon Buddhist sect, is Japan's most memorable graveyard walkway. It's the approach to the *oku-no-in* (inner sanctuary) where stands the mausoleum of Kukai, founder of Shingon Buddhism in the ninth century. The path winds through a forest lined with mossy tombs of Muromachi-era generals and daimyo lords. In beams of pale light shimmering through the trees, you can barely pick out age-worn inscriptions on the monuments of the once mighty. It's the most mysterious and numinous place on Mount Koya.

When I visit an old graveyard, shaded by tall trees, tombstones nestled amongst weeds and fallen leaves, and overgrown by moss, I sense the presence of old spirits. One aspect of Japan's traditional love of stones is that their texture was always somewhat rough. In many cases, the carvers left chisel marks clearly viewable on the surface. Even the most delicately carved Buddhist stone lanterns would have an element of this roughness, and it's this that allowed for rain and wind to penetrate the surface, for moss and lichens to grow, for the stones to merge slowly with their natural surroundings. Raw stone was the very hallmark of Japan's stone culture, and this willingness to "just let stone be" had a huge influence on modern sculptors.

That ethos is vanishing, as Japan now favors machine-polished white granite. You see shiny granite and alabaster not only where you would expect it, around buildings in big cities, but in newly built stairs at temples and shrines, and most strikingly in tombstones. Bright tombstones, polished with industrial technology so as to shine forever, are now the standard, and they are starting to invade even the graveyards of Mount Koya. When I stand in front of one of these, it feels that the glossy surface is too shiny for spirits; they've bounced off the impermeable stone and fled upward into the sky. The appeal of the Jewish Cemetery and the older parts of Mount Koya is that the spirits are still there.

One good thing about Tokoji is that tourists to Hagi mostly don't seem to know about it. At the time of our visit, Tokoji was nearly empty. Standing amongst those rows of moss-covered stone lanterns one could feel the sorrowful march of time.

Curving walls and a waterway

We finally arrived at our main objective, the castle town of Hagi. Before coming here I had seen many picturesque photographs of the town. Japan has numerous places that call themselves Little Kyoto, but when you go there, you usually discover that the preserved old neighborhoods consist of just a few blocks. I expected that if we had thirty minutes to an hour, we should be able to see Hagi. But after arrival, we realized that the old town of covers a considerable area, far more extensive than either Kyoto's Gion or Kanazawa's Sanchayagai.

The old areas of Kanazawa and Kyoto are overshadowed by the modern cityscapes that enfold them, barely daring to raise their heads next to their bright high-rising neighbors. In Hagi there's a critical density of old neighborhoods in close proximity: the Edoya Yokocho area, the Horiuchi area near the castle ruins, and the houses lining Aibagawa stream. The newer parts of town surrounding them are still somewhat old-fashioned, low height, with not much large-scale development, and so in Hagi the illusion that you are walking the streets of an unchanged old city works. You have slipped back in time.

One of my pleasures in walking around towns like Hagi lies in old *shirakabe*, earthen walls coated with white plaster. In Hagi, from small houses up to large institutions such as schools, shirakabe surround everything. An unusual facet of these walls is that when viewed as a cross-section from the side, they are not rectangular or trapezoidal, as most walls in Japan are, but curve upward and outward, like the plectrum of a shamisen.

The first time I saw walls like this was in the samurai neighborhood of Taketa City in Oita Prefecture in central Kyushu. I suppose they must have an official name, but I call them *bachigata* "plectrum walls," because they look like the flaring ivory *bachi* plectrum used to strum a shamisen. Finding bachigata walls in Hagi made me wonder what the connections might have been between Yamaguchi and Kyushu during the Muromachi era. Maybe bachi-shaped walls also exist in other places, but they certainly give a distinctive look to the streets of old Hagi.

Another charming aspect of Hagi was the samurai houses lining Aibagawa stream. Like the Shakemachi neighborhood of Kamigamo Shrine in Kyoto, the houses stand on the stream bank and are entered via big slabs of stone laid across the waterway. One of the houses, Kyu-Yukawake Residence, is open to the public. Inside there's a sunken kitchen, lowered halfway down to the level of the stream, from which water flows right into the kitchen.

When you walk through a town like this there's much to see and

Bachigata "plectrum-shaped" concave plaster walls

feel—in the curve of a wall, in the stone slabs crossing a stream. We explored as much of Hagi's old neighborhoods as we could, but far from being done in an hour, we could easily have spent a week in Hagi and still not have encompassed it all.

The "finger-pointing" castle

A castle town by its very name centers on its castle, and we couldn't leave without seeing Hagi Castle. The old Shizuki Castle of the lords of Hagi was one of the many dismantled by order of the Meiji government in the 1870s. All that remains today is part of the moats and the stone walls. The slope of the wall enclosing the section where the main tower once stood makes a graceful curve. Reflected in the water of the moat, it's the reverse of the rising Mount Fuji–like lines of Shizuki-yama Hill just behind it.

Usually there would be more visitors at Shizuki, but at the time we visited, just before dusk, there was nobody at all and the grounds were infused with supernal quiet.

The name Shizuki means "finger pointing at the moon." The Tang dynasty monk Fayan is said to have preached a koan (a riddle for Zen

The ruins of Hagi Castle, and Shizuki-yama Hill

meditation): "With my finger I point at the moon, the finger is not the moon."[1] This means "The teachings of sages only aim at enlightenment, they are not enlightenment itself." Another way to interpret these words is: the moon that we can never actually touch, that is, enlightenment, is forever beyond our reach. This famous phrase would certainly have been known to the lord of Choshu who built this castle. In the name "Shizuki," used for both the mountain and the castle, there's a poetic mood of innocent enjoyment of the moon. One can imagine the lord pointing to the moon during a drinking party beside the moat. It could be as simple as that. Yet the lord would also have been aware that this name is a koan, and as such is infused deeply with Zen philosophy. The castle disappeared a century and a half ago, but the moats and walls still have something to tell us.

Fresh green in untouched mountains

Travel in the countryside is hardly all about cultural relics. It can also be a quest for nature, sometimes in the form of "agricultural parkland"

1.「以指指月指非月」

which man has created in rice terraces and fields, and other times in untamed nature itself in mountains and along seacoasts.

From Hagi we set out driving north to see the seaside cliffs of Susa Hornfels dating back fourteen million years. "Hornfels" is hardly a word most of us would be familiar with, as it's a geological term referring to a type of hard metamorphic rock with strong white and black stripes. These are created by overlays of sandstone and mudstone baked together by the heat of volcanic magma. The hornfels cliffs along the sea at Susa have been eroded by wind and water revealing a cleft surface showing dramatic stripes.

It was a thirty-minute drive from Hagi to get there but the roads were almost empty. Our objective was the Susa Hornfels, but my eye was drawn to the mountains that we drove through on the way. As it had been in Amami, there were very few *sugi* cryptomeria cedar plantations, so the mountains had the fluffy rounded look of Japan's virgin forest. It was May, the season of *shinryoku* "new green," but the mountains were rich in many colors; we saw tints of light brown, red and pink, greens of various shades and yellow.

In Japan we hear the term shinryoku used to describe the fresh foliage of spring. But before the leaves settle down to the darker greens of summer, the fresh new leaf buds in fact turn a spectrum of colors as they sprout and mature. Depending on their species, many trees flower with tiny blooms covering them from top to bottom. In some places it looked like the mountainsides were covered in drifts of snow tinted yellow and pale green.

In this rich season of new green, I was impressed once more with the abundance of Japan's natural forests. The Hagi area, at least along the coast, seems to have escaped the worst of industrial forestry. Around the more southerly part of Yamaguchi Prefecture near Nagato City, one starts to see more sugi plantations, but in general they seem less extensive in Yamaguchi than in most other parts of Honshu, Shikoku and Kyushu. One wonders why.

The future of the Susa Hornfels cliffs

Returning to the Susa Hornfels. The scale is not large, but it's a rare and wonderful landscape. When we visited we saw only a few other people there, but along the highway from where you walk down to the hornfels cliff, there's a large bus parking lot. There's nothing inherently bad in parking lots, but this way danger lies.

In the *Kanko Rikkoku* "Build Up the Nation with Tourism" boom of the last few years, there's been a dramatic increase of foreign tourists—who are followed closely by domestic tourists once they read that a place has become internationally famous. In this era of over-tourism, the cliffs of Susa are in fact fragile, exposed to the threat of so-called tourist pollution.

For example, the famous cliffs and rocks of Tojinbo in Fukui Prefecture are one of nature's wonders. But the viewpoint above is encrusted with uncontrolled development. The beauty of the place fades in the shadow of shabby tourist facilities.

In Japan's "construction state," as tourist demand grows, this leads to a new spate of public works projects. In the name of catering to an expected flood of foreign tourists, bureaucrats carve highways out of mountains and flatten cliffsides with cement, while billboards and other signage proliferates.

Recent decades have seen an obsession with "safety," resulting in bright signage everywhere warning of "danger," and shiny railings even along rice paddies in small villages. Luckily, on and around the Susa Hornfels there are so far no guardrails and the rest of the construction and clutter, but as tourists increase, one can well imagine what might happen next.

The Susa Hornfels are quiet enough right now, but won't always be. One would hope that Hagi and Susa would start to think of how they can manage these cliffs in the future. For example, the descent from the road to the hornfels cliffs had spots that were genuinely dangerous. At some point, as visitors increase, guardrails may in fact be necessary. How then could they be designed so as to fit in with the hornfels rocks, and not clash with them? Could tourist flow be

The Higashi Ushirobata rice terraces, Nagato City

controlled by regulations or reservation systems? All this before the tourist floods arrive in earnest. It's easy to foresee the ways in which this place can—and likely will—be degraded. All I can do is to pray that somehow the Susa Hornfels cliffs survive what's coming for them.

Seaside rice terraces and the Akiyoshidai plateau

Next we headed southwest of Hagi to the Higashi Ushirobata rice terraces of Nagato City. Spreading out along hillsides by the sea, they reminded me of the Shiroyone terraces of the Noto Peninsula, but the terrain is gentler here. It was just before the rice was planted, so a number of the paddies had water spread in them, reflecting the blue sky.

As well as at Higashi Ushirobata, we found beautiful rice paddies scattered throughout this region. Compared to Shiroyone they're still largely unknown, without tourist facilities, so they still have the feeling of untouched rural agriculture.

Not far from the rice terraces is Motonosumi Shrine, whose row of bright red *torii* gates descending a sleep slope down to the sea has become an international Instagram mecca. The torii make a dramatic social-media image, but when seen in its entirety the surroundings are not quite so photogenic. The neighboring hillside is compacted with plenty of concrete, with wide stretches of parking lot descending in flat levels—like cement rice terraces, one is tempted to think.

On the way back we drove along the "karst road," through the karst fields of the Akiyoshidai plateau. In 1971—half a century ago, when I think of it—I hitchhiked across Japan, and Akiyoshidai was one of the places that I visited. I was nineteen at the time. Perhaps because it's a national park, Akiyoshi is unchanged. It's exactly as I remember it.

Looking at the karst outcroppings with the eye of an older adult, I find myself comparing them to the standing stones of Sesshu's garden at Joeiji Temple. It's a wild conjecture, but I wonder if the model for Sesshu's garden might have come from Akiyoshidai's scattered stones. After all, he lived in Yamaguchi for several years and surely saw this landscape.

Akiyoshidai is Joeiji on a grand scale—a Sesshu garden before Sesshu. A case could be made that Sesshu duplicated the "Akiyoshidai effect" when returned to Kyoto and started designing gardens there. Afterward, this became the default mode for all of Japan's rock gardens. At Akiyoshidai, so perfect is the arrangement of each clump of "Sesshu stones" that I kept asking for the car to be stopped, somewhat to the annoyance of my traveling companions.

This is the magic of discovering in real life what one had supposed only existed in art. In Proust, Swann is obsessed by the similarity of the features of his beloved Odette to the rounded faces, wisps of golden hair and melancholy eyes in the paintings of Botticelli. Likewise, I found delight when, in Iya Valley in the 1970s, I first saw that the floating ribbons of mist drifting across the hills looked exactly like the strips of gold leaf that separate mountain views on painted screens. I had thought those bandings of gold leaf were just a handy technique to break up the painting space. But no, they're drawn from life. In Iya, the mists are even better than a painting of course, because they move.

Here at Akiyoshidai, it's rock garden after rock garden, each with stones that have been chosen by a master. Thousands of them, all different, all wonders of spatial setting. Who needs garden designers when we have this?

I imagine that it wasn't only Sesshu who was influenced back in the fifteenth century. It's possible that Shigemori Mirei also was inspired by these outcroppings in the twentieth century when he designed his craggy modern gardens.

Seeing Akiyoshidai perfectly preserved as it was decades ago, brings me a sense of unfettered joy. So few places in Japan have retained their pristine beauty, and this place has, on a grand scale. Driving for mile after mile under the blue skies of Akiyoshidai, past enigmatic stones reaching to the horizon, we head for Kyoto and home.

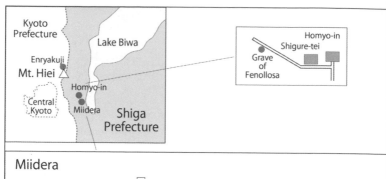

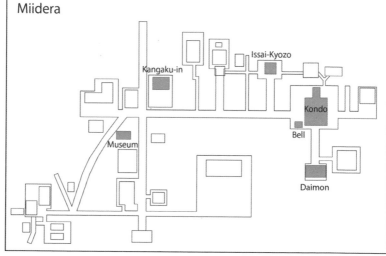

8

Esoteric Secrets
Miidera Temple, Shiga Prefecture

I n the search for hidden places it sometimes pays to return to a place that you've been to before. Just next door may lie further secrets. *Mikkyo* (Esoteric Buddhism) with its emphasis on rising levels of secrets lends itself to just such a search.

On this trip we returned to the neighborhood of Hiyoshi Taisha Shrine on the shores of Lake Biwa to the east of Kyoto. Hiyoshi had grown up as the guardian shrine of Enryakuji Temple, headquarters of Tendai Mikkyo on Mount Hiei. This time we visited another site also connected to Enryakuji, the temple of Miidera.

I've long had a personal interest in Miidera. Thirty years ago I did some research for an article I wrote about Ernest Fenollosa, the American art expert active in the early Meiji period, who revalued traditional Japanese art, and his student Okakura Tenshin. I learned that Miidera held deep meaning for them and that Fenollosa's bones were buried at a sub-temple of Miidera called Homyo-in. Fenollosa's quest for the essence of Japanese beauty had brought him here in the end.

Another reason for my interest was the poem cycle "Eight Views of Omi." Omi is the former name for Shiga Prefecture. In my collection of old calligraphies and paintings, there are several handscrolls on the theme of the "Eight Views of Omi." One of the poems is the *Evening Bell of Miidera*. My interest piqued by the Evening Bell, I studied more about Miidera and discovered that it's a treasure house of ancient Mikkyo art. Eventually I acquired many a book and illustrated catalogue of Miidera. Yet I had never visited.

Evening Bell at Miidera, seventeenth-century handscroll (Collection: Alex Kerr)

Miidera's history goes back to the Asuka period in the seventh century. However, its development into a great temple took place in the latter half of the ninth century under the influence of one of the monks of Mount Hiei, Enchin. It's said that he gave the temple its name.

A generation after the first abbot, Saicho, founded Enryakuji on the peak of Mount Hiei in 806, two monks from his lineage, Ennin (794–864) and Enchin (814–891), traveled to China, bringing back with them huge collections of Buddhist sutras and ritual implements, and it was under them that Tendai Buddhism began its expansion into becoming Japan's premier national religion. In later centuries, Zen, the Pure Land Amidist sects and Nichiren Buddhism all got their start within Tendai. Ennin was the third, and Enchin the fifth patriarch of Tendai.

At the death of Enchin in 891, Mount Hiei was riven into two factions supporting Ennin and Enchin. Their clashes grew increasingly violent until finally, in 993, the Enchin faction descended the mountain and established themselves at Miidera. From that time the monks at the peak of Mount Hiei were called the *sanmonha* "mountain faction," and the monks at Miidera the *jimonha* "temple faction." Thus began a violent struggle that continued for six hundred years. The monks of Enryakuji attacked and burned Miidera numerous times; history records at least sixty armed battles between the two factions.

What put an end to the struggle between the factions was the wrath of the two great warlords who unified Japan in the late sixteenth century, Oda Nobunaga and Toyotomi Hideyoshi. First came Nobunaga's devastating attack on Enryakuji in 1571. With its thousands of armed monks, Enryakuji had terrified the capital for centuries. The temple posed a military challenge to Nobunaga, and it had made the mistake of siding with anti-Nobunaga warlords and factions at court. Nobunaga decided to do away once and for all with the power of Mount Hiei. He ordered his troops to attack without mercy, and in one night they massacred all the monks, all the men, women and children living on the mountain, and burned the whole complex down.

Some years later Hideyoshi, in a fit of anger, also abolished Miidera, although his approach was milder than Nobunaga's. He issued an edict commanding the destruction of Miidera's temples, but he allowed the monks to live. Both temples were later revived, but greatly weakened; their rivalry was never a serious factor afterward. In the case of Miidera, near the end of his life, Hideyoshi, fearing the curse of the Miidera bodhisattvas, permitted the temple to be rebuilt. Later, under the Edo shogunate, Tokugawa Ieyasu supported the temple with the result that much Momoyama-era architecture still survives here.

Momoyama-era structures at Miidera Temple

Enryakuji suffered cataclysmic damage from being burned down in the space of one night, and thus saw almost all its ancient treasures destroyed. However Miidera had good warning. There was time to remove its art works and libraries to other locations before Hideyoshi's edict came into effect. Later on, when Miidera was rebuilt, these were returned to the temple, with the result that far more from antiquity was preserved. The reconstruction of Miidera took place a decade before Enryakuji was rebuilt, with feudal grandees from the Edo shogun on down involved, so buildings of huge importance were moved here. Today Miidera is one of Japan's preeminent repositories of Mikkyo art.

On arrival at Miidera we were met by the large late-sixteenth-century Daimon gate, once part of Hideyoshi's legendary Fushimi Castle on Momoyama Hill south of Kyoto, but dismantled and donated to Miidera by Tokugawa Ieyasu. Beginning with this gate, Miidera is a collection of fine Momoyama-era and early Edo-era buildings, donated by the great lords and ladies of the time—Hideyoshi's widow Kita-no-mandokoro; Ieyasu; and Mori Terumoto, Lord of Choshu—as well as old structures moved from distant sub-temples.

Among them, the Kondo Hall donated by Kita-no-mandokoro is one of the most splendid Momoyama buildings in existence and is designated a National Treasure. It puts across the unique feeling of high Momoyama: expansive and strong, yet delicate and light.

The exquisite Kondo Hall was built in 1599, right in the last year of Momoyama. But the date 1599 is just a number. This temple hall rises above its time; it's simply a masterpiece. The Momoyama era was a magic moment in human culture. As with the Renaissance, one can say that few things this fine were created before or since.

Inside the Kondo Hall are many important Buddhist sculptures, but it was quite surprising to find here also a number of the crude and abstract works of the seventeenth-century monk-sculptor Enku. Far from the gilt and polish of Buddhist art as found in Kyoto, Enku worked with raw chunks of wood. A slash here, and a chip there, and a quirky bodhisattva would appear. A hermit who lived most of his life immured in the villages of Gifu Prefecture, Enku was known to have avoided the centers of Buddhist authority, especially around Kyoto.

Stoic Enku is the last person one expects to find surrounded by Momoyama gorgeousness. And for him, one suspects, the gorgeousness was incidental. We know that Enku made an effort to visit places he thought were sources of spiritual secrets, such as ancient Horyuji

The Evening Bell of Miidera

Temple near Nara. It seems Enku was drawn to the mystical Mikkyo teachings of Miidera, and this is why he visited and kept up relations.

Standing on the other side of the Kondo courtyard is the pavilion housing the Evening Bell of Miidera. Although small, this too is a Momoyama building. For a few hundred yen you can strike it and hear its famous sound. It not being evening, I refrained. That night, staying at a lakeside hotel, I imagined how that bell must have echoed over Lake Biwa in the old days.

The mysteries of Mikkyo

Further on into the Miidera complex is the Issai Kyozo Hall of All of the Sutras. This building was donated in the early Edo period by Mori Terumoto, Lord of Choshu, and brought from Yamaguchi. An Issai Kyozo is a distinctive edifice found in Mikkyo temples. It's basically an empty hall erected to shelter a hexagonal structure called a *rinzo* "revolving repository." The rinzo is filled from bottom to top with drawers and shelves containing the full set of Buddhist scriptures.

The hexagonal rinzo stands on a central pillar which is affixed to the roof and the floor, around which it revolves. To rotate the rinzo is to spread the divine words written in the scriptures into the air until they penetrate the whole world, bringing merit to all sentient beings, and of course also to the person doing the rotating.

Similar revolving sutra repositories can be seen in temples around Japan, notably in Kyoto at Ninnaji and Seiryoji temples. Nor is this limited to Japan. Examples can be found in China from Beijing to Tibet. The belief that one gains merit by rotating papers on which the words of the sutras are written spread from Tibet across the Himalayas.

At the time we visited Miidera, I was working on my book *Finding the Heart Sutra* (2020). Shortest of all Buddhist scriptures, the Heart Sutra is thought to express the condensed essence of all Buddhist teachings. Zen loves it because it's sharp, bizarre and paradoxical. Mikkyo (both in Japan and in Tibet) loves it because it's rich in secrets. The Heart Sutra is like a "treasure lake" in which precious texts of lost wisdom lie submerged, waiting to be found.

The Heart Sutra ends with a sacred mantra whose opening words are *Gyatei, gyatei*. These and the following syllables of the mantra have no apparent meaning in and of themselves, being pure mystical sound. Yet they have been thought since ancient times to bring spiritual power to both the person who recites it and those who hear it. The rotating of a rinzo, spreading blessings in the world and the reciting of the *Gyatei, gyatei* mantra are similar in their spiritual effects.

But in talking about the Heart Sutra's mantra I run up against the skepticism of modern times. Is the spiritual power of the *Gyatei, gyatei* mantra just superstition, or does it reflect something deeper in the universe? Likewise, what does the turning of a rinzo really do? Traditionally, it was believed that Mikkyo rituals had cosmic force; with them you could literally change the world. I raise these questions, but leave them here as a Mikkyo mysteries.

From the latter twentieth century, most Westerners interested in things Japanese have focused on Zen, with its stripped-down art forms and live-in-the-moment philosophy. But the foreigners active in Japan in the nineteenth century, like Fenollosa, were drawn less to Zen and more to esoteric Mikkyo, especially to Tendai. Earlier, so was the weirdly abstract sculptor Enku. And for similar reasons. Mikkyo is closely related to the mystical world of Tibetan Buddhism. In contrast to minimalistic Zen, it's rich in symbolism, iconography and ancient rituals going back to pre-Buddhist Brahmanic India. Rather than living in the moment, the ultimate mysteries lie far beyond this moment, to be glimpsed slowly, in ascending levels of initiation.

Arriving in Japan soon after it opened up to the outside world at the end of the nineteenth century, Fenollosa and his friends were on a voyage of discovery into an unknown country, and they found its deep secrets in Tendai Mikkyo.

The art of Kano Mitsunobu

With my interest in folding screens and *fusuma* sliding doors, I hoped to see the famous paintings on the doors and in the *tokonoma* alcove of the Kangaku-in reception hall. Painted by Kano Mitsunobu, son of the great Momoyama-era painter Kano Eitoku, in 1600, these are considered to be one of the jewels of Momoyama painting.

From the fifteenth century, Japan's painters were divided into lineages, such as the Kano, Tosa and Unkoku schools, (the latter descended from Sesshu). Kano and Unkoku painted in a highly Chinese way, with soaring mountains, picturesque tree branches, fast-flowing water and so forth. This is called *karayo* "Chinese style."

The Tosa school tended toward portrayal of scenes from courtly novels, and delicate images of grasses and wildflowers. This was called *wayo* "Japanese style," an echo of the karayo–wayo distinction that we saw in Chapter 3 with regard to roofs: tiled was karayo; thatched, or roofed with laminated bark, was wayo. In paintings, high peaks and luscious flowers like peonies were karayo; soft hills and wildflowers were wayo.

By the Momoyama era, when the great lords were building their extravagant castles, the Kano school had swept all before it. To the techniques of Chinese ink painting, the Kano artists brought lavish use of color and dynamic movement on a grand scale. While the other schools lived on, and many other schools developed during Edo, the Kano school remained paramount for four hundred years.

Although a Kano, Mitsunobu followed a path of his own, with a unique synthesis of karayo and wayo. Mitsunobu brought the techniques of Yamato-e "Japanese images," with gentle mountains and a childlike love of grasses and wildflowers, to his painting style, creating a fresh and lively hybrid between karayo and Yamato-e. Hardly any Momoyama painting could be called more beautiful than his.

The Kangaku-in reception hall is usually closed to the public, and was under total restoration at the time we visited. Luckily all the paintings have been removed to the temple's museum and are on view there. On completion of the restoration, they'll place facsimiles in the Kangaku-in, and the originals will stay permanently in the museum.

Momoyama-era and early Edo-era painting is poorly known, not only among foreigners, but even among the Japanese. Many temples with classic works are closed to the public, and even if they sometimes allow viewings, they don't permit photography. So most people have no chance to see or study these things. It's a fact of modern life that what isn't photographed and visible on the Internet might as well not exist. It disappears from the cultural record. Also, as these paintings on paper are fragile and easily damaged by sunlight, originals are often kept in storage, and facsimiles installed in their place.

Part of the appeal of Momoyama painting is that you can appreciate the passage of time with the aging of the gold leaf. Also, the pigments were made from ground minerals that flake or bleach with time, producing the *wabi* (humble and low key) and *sabi* (worn and weathered) atmosphere so prized in the past.

The most prominent feature of age is *hakuashi* "gold-leaf footprints," a result of the faint tarnishing that takes places at the seams and overlaps of squares of gold leaf. While over 99 percent pure, slight imperfections in the gold leaf show themselves after hundreds of years.

Unfortunately, the new facsimiles lean to a "brand new" look, brightly colored and reflective. With modern technology, they can now make replicas displaying the faint marks of age and texture of silk and paper, which are so accurate that you can stand within inches and hardly tell them from the original. This alternative exists, and some temples have installed such facsimiles with success. However, by and large the authorities in charge of temples and palaces prefer the gloss of freshly painted new copies. It's related to the polish of modern Japanese stone, which has replaced the raw semifinished stone of traditional times. The emphasis in both cases is on permanence and shine. Appreciation of wabi and sabi have been much admired ideals in the literature about Japan. Sadly, it would be hard to find wabi-sabi in the interiors of temples and castles redecorated with the new facsimiles. Visitors seeing these copies will never guess that Japanese classical art was ever deeper than this.

I'd like to pause here and say a few words about the contrasts I've been remarking on throughout this book (old paintings with delicate shadings of ink and gold leaf, versus bright restorations; rocky seashores versus concrete embankments; natural forest versus industrial "*sugi* deserts"). It would be easy to see what I've written as the grumbling of an old timer, obsessed with how much better it was in the old days. And indeed, I am deeply disturbed by these changes since they run so much against the Japan I loved since childhood. Nevertheless, one might wonder what use it is to describe things are no longer there, since people living in or visiting Japan today can no longer see them.

But in fact you can still see them. Lush natural forests, rough-carved stones, and the rest, do still exist. But nowadays you need an extra stock of knowledge to seek out "what's real." With that knowledge, when you find the real thing, your joy is tripled; and when you don't find it, there's satisfaction in understanding what you're looking at.

Some Japan lovers are leery of this knowledge because they fear it will somehow turn them against Japan. But actually it's the key to the secret garden. My purpose in writing *Hidden Japan* is as a sort of treasure map. Follow the clues and you'll know what to look for.

I have no idea how the replicas of the paintings at Kangaku-in will turn out once the restoration is completed, but it might not much matter because the originals can be viewed at any time at the museum. This is not the case, sadly, at Nijo Castle in Kyoto, where the originals are stored in a building on the grounds, but rarely shown to the public. It's a thing to be grateful for at Miidera that these glorious masterworks are on display. For anyone interested in the depth of expression in Japanese classical painting, I would recommend a visit to the Miidera museum.

Ernest Fenollosa and Miidera

The young Bostonian Ernest Fenollosa arrived in Japan in 1878, aged twenty-five, and soon was teaching at Tokyo Imperial University. With the *haibutsu kishaku* anti-Buddhist movement still raging, people were tearing down pagodas and throwing Buddhist statues into the flames. Japan, long split into hundreds of feudal fiefs, was not yet a unified state. There were many dark corners, with temples harboring "secret Buddhas" that hadn't been seen for hundreds of years. The government realized that they simply didn't know what was out there. At the request of the authorities, Fenollosa traveled to Nara and other places in Japan to research the state of Japan's ancient art heritage.

At the time, the techniques of oil painting and theories of Western art had delivered a profound shock to Japan, and the trend was to look down on traditional Japanese art. Fenollosa, in opposition to this, called for a rediscovery of old arts such as calligraphy and Kano-school painting. His 1882 lecture "An Explanation of the Truth of Art" had a wide influence on the Japanese art world. His influential disciples included playwright Tsubouchi Shoyo and art critic Okakura Tenshin.

Okakura Tenshin

Ernest Fenollosa

William Sturgis Bigelow

In 1890 Fenollosa returned to America, becoming curator of Japanese art at the Museum of Fine Arts Boston (MFA). Okakura Tenshin followed in his footsteps, succeeding him as curator at the MFA. Tenshin's *The Book of Tea* (1906), introducing Japanese aesthetics to the West, is a modern classic still in print more than a century later.

Fenollosa was also an art collector who acquired pieces that would today be listed as National Treasures. He inspired a group of wealthy Bostonians to come to Japan and helped them to build their own collections, which contributed to the spread of knowledge of Japanese art throughout the world. One of them, William Sturgis Bigelow, was a director of the MFA, and became Fenollosa and Tenshin's patron. Thanks to Fenollosa's acquisitions and donations by Bigelow and his friends, today the MFA boasts the most important collection of Japanese art outside of Japan.

One story widely recounted in the Japanese art world concerns a visit that Fenollosa, Bigelow and Tenshin paid to Nara. With the special permission of the government, they gained access to hidden temple premises and were able to inspect artworks unseen for centuries. One of their visits was to the Shosoin Treasury, which had remained a closed time capsule ever since Emperor Shomu's relics were stored there in the mid-eighth century. The custodians gave Fenollosa's group a few shards of ancient pottery, which Bigelow later gifted to the MFA. To this day these are the only pieces which have ever been taken abroad from the Shosoin.

Fenollosa and Tenshin were employed by the Imperial Museum in Tokyo (precursor of the Tokyo National Museum). The museum's director was a former samurai from Satsuma Fief in southern Kyushu by the name of Machida Hisanari. Deeply religious, Machida was drawn to the Mikkyo of Miidera and introduced Fenollosa and Tenshin to Miidera's sub-temple of Homyo-in. Fenollosa, Bigelow and Tenshin received initiation there together, and took Buddhist names. Fenollosa was Taishin, "Heart of the Precepts"; Bigelow was Gesshin, "Heart of the Moon"; and Tenshin was Sesshin, "Heart of Snow."

In later years Fenollosa and Bigelow rented an outer building of Homyo-in called Shigure-tei "Pavilion of Autumn Rain," visiting there from time and time, spending their days reading books and studying Tendai Buddhism. Fenollosa died in 1908 while on a trip to London, and according to his wishes, his bones were interred at Homyo-in. Bigelow died in 1926 and had his tombstone erected at Homyo-in too.

The foreigners drawn to Japanese art

Homyo-in is nestled in the hills, separated a way from the main complex of Miidera. Residential development is swallowing up the hill, making the temple rather hard to find. After circling around a few times finally we identified the entryway, overgrown with grass, seemingly deserted. Ahead of us we saw a flight of old stone stairs, and at the top of it was Homyo-in.

The Shigure-tei Pavilion, located just to the side of Homyo-in, still exists, but in decayed condition. Peeking inside we saw some old mildewed books lying scattered around. Could these have belonged to Fenollosa? Its garden overlooks a wide view of Lake Biwa, and one imagines that this was enjoyed by Fenollosa and Bigelow when they stayed here. From the garden another path rose into the forest and we arrived at a graveyard dotted with tombs. It was a chilly day with a light drizzle, and we were the only people here. The place was utterly silent.

As we walked past mossy tombstones covered with fallen leaves, we found the resting places of Fenollosa and Bigelow. Reading the inscription on Fenollosa's monument, I saw to my surprise that the stone lanterns were gifted by Charles Freer, who in 1906 donated his massive collection of Chinese and Japanese art to the Smithsonian Museum in Washington DC. The Freer Gallery of Art boasts the second most important collection of Japanese art in America. In the quiet of Homyo-in, the names of the three American giants of Japanese art in the late nineteenth and early twentieth centuries are to be found together.

Another person should be here. Where was Machida Hisanari, first director of the Imperial Museum, who had brought these foreigners to Miidera? After a bit of looking around, we found his tombstone too. In the end only one of the group had gone a separate way, Okakura Tenshin. The others, Fenollosa, Bigelow and Machida all sleep here at Homyo-in.

Enchin and art collectors

In the history of Japanese art in the West since the nineteenth century, there are a number of important foreign collectors. Among them were people like Mary Burke who left much of her collection to the Metropolitan Museum of New York in 2015, and Etsuko and Joe Price who in 2020 sold their major collection to the Idemitsu Museum in Tokyo. While on a much more modest scale, I've also devoted myself to collecting Japanese art, and this has led me to study Zen and Mikkyo.

The foreign collections of Japanese art now housed in museums across the world can be traced back to the legacy of Fenollosa, Bigelow and Freer. But long before the foreigners bought their first pieces from Japan in the late nineteenth century, the Japanese themselves had been avid collectors of beautiful objects from abroad for a thousand years.

In the eighth century, the emperors and their courts in Nara collected widely from across Asia, as we know from the Shosoin Treasury, from which Fenollosa and Bigelow took shards to Boston. Emperor Shomu's trove of screens, scrolls, ceramics, musical instruments, lacquerware, gold and silver artifacts, and much more sealed inside the Shosoin in 756 might be the world's greatest ancient stash of collected art. It's filled to the overflowing with treasure from Tang-dynasty China, Mongolia, the Silk Road and beyond.

The gate of the Shigure-tei Pavilion

A century later, when Enchin returned from China with hundreds of sculptures, paintings, and gilded bronze implements, he was following a Japanese thirst for collection from overseas that long preceded him. The Japanese never stopped buying art from China, but in later centuries it was mostly brought in on merchant ships. The few Japanese travelers who did venture into Yuan or Ming China didn't have the financial resources of the imperial court or a wealthy temple like Enryakuji behind them. This makes Enchin, while hardly the first or last, one of the greatest Japanese amassers of foreign art, placing Miidera firmly in the mainstream of Japanese art collecting. It's condign karma that the early foreign collectors would be drawn to this place.

Amassing cultural items from neighboring kingdoms is hardly unusual. The Romans filled their villas with Greek sculptures; the Thais installed Khmer statues in their glittering capital of Ayutthaya. But most of it was acquired by war and conquest. Or sometimes dug up out of ruins. The Japanese, in contrast, bought and paid for it all. In the centuries after Enchin, junks from China and southeast Asia ferried art treasures to a country where they knew these things would be valued by knowledgeable collectors and paid for in gold. The sale of art (mostly one way, from China to Japan) picked up steam after the late 1300s when the shoguns, made wealthy by trade with the Ming dynasty, avidly collected all things Chinese. Even after Japan closed itself to the outside world in 1603, Chinese junks were still allowed to trade at the port of Nagasaki in the south, and when they arrived, they were met by art dealers waiting at the dock. Japan was Asia's first bona fide international art market.

Once purchased, the Japanese owners sequestered their art treasures in temples such as Miidera, or storehouses such as the Shosoin, and threw away the keys. In the shadowy interiors of these sacred places, art which is now lost in the rest of the Asia survived a millennium of upheavals.

The Asian collecting went on, right up until the 1930s, after which attention shifted to the West, with the Japanese buying up Monets and Picassos. Today no other Asian nation has such rich collections of art from other cultures beside their own. In Beijing and Shanghai you can see a lot of Chinese art; hardly any Japanese or European; a similar thing could be said about Seoul or Bangkok. With so much effort and money having gone into collecting from overseas, Japan overflows with art from across the world. Fenollosa, Bigelow and Freer did a little to redress the balance.

In addition to the collectors, I noticed that there's another foreigner's tomb at Homyo-in. Reading the barely legible placard, I made out that it was the memorial of the Harvard scholar James Woods. The placard notes that Woods was a sutra researcher, specializing in Mikkyo and the Yoga Sutra. I've spent many years studying the Heart Sutra and finally wrote a book about it. I feel that makes me also a sutra researcher. When I think about it, first Enchin long ago, and then Machida, Fenollosa, and the rest, only collected or curated art as a sideline. First and foremost, they were in search of Mikkyo secrets; that is, they were all sutra researchers. The same could probably be said about the sculptor Enku.

Lately I've given some thought to where I might like to buried in Japan. Gazing upon the tombstones of Fenollosa, Bigelow and Woods, I find myself thinking, "I wouldn't mind ending up with them."

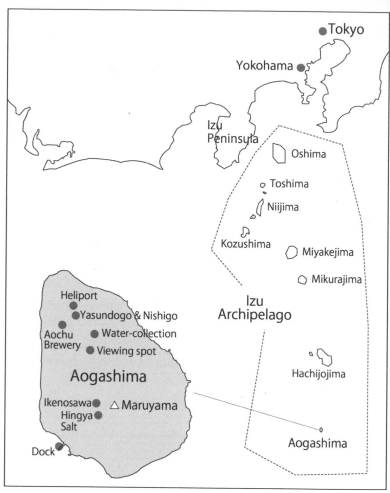

Tokyo

Yokohama

Izu
Peninsula

Oshima

Toshima

Niijima

Kozushima

Miyakejima

Mikurajima

Izu
Archipelago

Heliport

Yasundogo & Nishigo

Aochu
Brewery

Water-collection

Viewing spot

Aogashima

Ikenosawa

Hingya
Salt

△ Maruyama

Hachijojima

Dock

Aogashima

9

Living on a Volcano
Aogashima Island, Tokyo Municipality

I n my library there's a prized book about remote islands by German author Judith Schalansky entitled *Pocket Atlas of Remote Islands: Fifty Islands I Have Not Visited and Never Will.*

In it are nautical maps of islands in the middle of the Pacific, the Atlantic, near the North Pole and so on. The maps show only seacoasts and some basic place names; otherwise, there's no sense of geography or landscape. Schalansky writes a couple of pages with an anecdote or two about each place, and these short accounts flesh out what we don't see on the simple maps. I've read and reread this book and each time it gets me dreaming.

Japan has plenty of romantic islands. Okinoshima, Sado, Iki, the Ogasawara Islands, Amami and Yakushima are just a few of the better-known ones. I've been fortunate to visit Amami and Okinoshima, but there are hundreds of islands I've never traveled to. Of these, there was one island—the ultimate island—that I had long desired to visit: Aogashima.

Island of fantasy

By a fluke of history, Aogashima belongs to the Municipality of Tokyo's Island Department. This covers the many islands of the Izu archipelago, stretching from the Izu Peninsula far south and east into the Pacific Ocean. Aogashima lies fully 217 miles (350 km) away from Tokyo, at about the same longitude as Miyazaki in Kyushu. The first time I saw an aerial photograph of Aogashima I was immediately struck by it.

At 2 miles (3.5 km) north to south and 1½ miles (2.5 km) east to west, Aogashima's total land area comes to just over 2 square miles (6 km²). Completely surrounded by sheer cliffs rising from the sea, the island is a double caldera made up of two concentric volcanic cones: an outer ring of sea cliffs and an inner cone called Maruyama. Perfect double calderas like this are a rare sight, and with its remoteness, and surrounded by forbidding precipices, Aogashima is truly a fantasy island.

Access is difficult to the degree that there's an old saying, "Only with the help of the gods will you ever get there." Unless you have a very good reason to visit, it's not an easy thing to go to Aogashima. For a number of years I dreamed of this island like the ones in Schalansky's book as a place that "I have not visited and never will."

In 2017 I was appointed as a member of one of Tokyo Municipality's committees working with tourism. It was the Tokyo *Takarajima* (Treasure Islands) Committee whose focus is the islands of the Island Department. In the process I learned a lot about the Izu archipelago.

I already knew of the so-called Seven Islands of Izu, which are, counting from the closest to the Japanese mainland: Izu Oshima, Toshima, Niijima, Kozushima, Miyakejima, Mikurajima and finally Hachijojima, 174 miles (280 km) out at sea. I didn't know there were many more islands in the Island Department than I ever imagined, most of them islets and shoals, spread out over vast stretches of ocean. All have different geographies and weather patterns. A further 43 miles (70 km) south of Hachijojima—too remote to be counted as one of the Seven Islands—is Aogashima.

One could think of the Izu Islands as stepping stones, such as one sees in Japanese gardens, with Aogashima being the next to last one. From there it's one giant step, 373 miles (600 km), to the most southerly group, the Ogasawara Islands, which sit at the latitude of Okinawa. All the islands come under the jurisdiction of Tokyo, so no matter how far away they are, all the cars carry license plates marked Shinagawa, a district in southeast Tokyo. It's probably because the ferries to the islands depart from the port of Shinagawa.

From exile to tourism

As hardly needs saying, Japan is an island nation, comprising over 6,800 islands. Of these about 300 are inhabited. Nowadays when we speak of small islands, it conjures up images of leisure, lovely beaches and even a sense of *kawaii* cuteness. But in the old days the struggle for survival on these islands was harsh and people saw them rather as places of misery and hardship. From this came the idea of exiling criminals to islands as punishment.

Island exile was originally applied to political prisoners of high status such as emperors, court nobles and feudal lords. In the Edo period it expanded to a wide range of criminals from murderers down to minor felons such as gamblers. Fiefs would set aside a particular island to send their criminals to. Satsuma Fief dispatched offenders to Amami and Okinawa; Owari Fief sent them to Shinojima; Fukuoka Fief, to Genkaijima. The practice of island exile continued on a nationwide scale right up until 1908, when it was finally abolished.

Sado is Japan's most famous prison island, where the shogunate sent criminals to labor in the gold mines. But as a matter of fact, far more criminals were exiled to the islands of the Izu archipelago, which were a special kind of domain ruled not by a daimyo lord but directly by the shogun's officials in Edo. Prisoners on other exile islands were sent from their respective fiefs; prisoners sent to the Izu Islands came from all over Japan. According to materials preserved in Hachijojima's historical museum, during the Edo period Miyakejima received 2,300 people; Hachijojima 1,865; Oshima 150; Niijima 1,333; Kozushima 813; Mikurajima 50; while remote Aogashima received 6 people.

After World War II, this dark history was largely forgotten. For a few decades Hachijojima flourished as a resort destination, being called "Japan's Hawaii." But distant Aogashima never enjoyed any of the tourist flow, and so it remains today.

The aim of the Tokyo Takarajima Committee was to find ways to further tourism in the Izu Islands. One day they asked me if I would be willing to make a study trip to Aogashima and I leapt at the chance. And so, in October of 2019, I finally stepped foot on the island.

The ferry ride from Hachijojima

Even with the municipality's backing, it isn't easy to get from Tokyo to Aogashima. First you need to fly to Hachijojima, and from there take a ferry or a helicopter. Due to the vagaries of the weather, the ferries often cancel, with a departure rate of just 50 percent. Even if the weather is sunny, when there are high winds the ferries don't sail. The helicopter has space for only nine people, and as it also serves the islanders, it's not easy for outsiders to book a seat. And, like the ferry, the helicopter often cancels as well.

We flew from Haneda airport to Hachijojima, and from there transferred to the ferry terminal and waited. The ferries on the previous day, and the day before that, had canceled—and today it was raining. A ferry departure looked unlikely. We had booked a return flight on the helicopter for the next day, and there was no give in the schedule. If we missed the ferry, the helicopter reservations would be automatically canceled and the whole trip would be down the drain.

After a stressful wait, it was announced that the ferry would be departing. There are few times in my life I've looked forward to the approach to a place with such expectation. Sailing to Aogashima was

Approaching Aogashima Island

Aogashima's water-collection facility

on a par with landing by plane in Tahiti, or arrival by boat at the Piazza di San Marco in Venice.

The ferry slipped through a smooth gray sea for three hours, the view consisting of drizzle and mists to an empty horizon. Then we saw rise up out of the sea the red rock cliffs of Aogashima towering vertically 328 feet (100 meters). From the ferry we could see nothing at all of the interior.

We'd heard that if the waves were too high when the ferry arrived at the dock, the boat would turn around without attempting a dangerous landing. According to one of the Takarajima Committee members, exactly that had happened when a delegation from Tokyo came a few months ago. They had to return to Hachijojima. Luckily for us, the seas were calm, and our ferry was tethered to the dock with no incident.

At the dock, we transferred to a van which drove up a steep curving incline carved into the cliff which brought us into the interior of the island. Driving along the inside of the outer caldera through lush semitropical scenery, we reached a plateau near the northern point. There are two hamlets here called Yasundogo and Nishigo, and this is where most of the 170 residents of the island live.

We checked into our lodgings, a guesthouse called Aogashima-ya, run by the mayor's wife, dropped our bags and drove to a broad slanting mountain face not far from the inn. We had glimpsed it from the ferry while still at sea, an expanse of greenish-blue and couldn't figure out what it was. Up close we saw that the entire hillside was coated with smooth sheets of cement painted greenish-blue. Rain falling on the slope runs into channels leading to a large reservoir. The biggest problem on a small island like this is water. Aogashima has no streams or rivers. This rain-catching mountain slope is the island's most important facility.

From here we walked further up the hill for about five minutes to a viewing spot.

At the lip of the caldera

The view reminded me of the famous Nuuanu Pali Lookout on Hawaii's Oahu Island. The Pali is a sheer cliff on the northern edge of the mountain range running through central Oahu. On the drive up there via the winding road from Honolulu in the south, you see only a series of gentle green valleys. Then, when you reach the Pali Lookout, suddenly, before your eyes, the cliff drops sharply away, revealing emerald mountains marching off into the distance and a wide bay.

The viewing point at Aogashima stands atop the lip of the outer caldera, and as at the Pali Lookout, you see nothing until you reach the edge, and then the whole island opens up before you. In the middle is the inner caldera of Maruyama, forested with distinctive vertical tree plantings looking like pleats on a dress. At the moment we reached the viewing point, the rain paused and we could see mists floating over the rich forests below.

From here we descended into the valley toward Maruyama. Along the way we could see mist rising from depressions here and there. "Lovely mist," I murmured, only to be corrected by one of people

The interior of Aogashima

from Aogashima accompanying our group. "No," he said, "that's steam rising from the ground." The most recent volcanic eruption recorded at Aogashima was in 1785 which was over two centuries ago, but the western side of Maruyama still exudes steam and there are bare areas where plants won't grow.

Steamed salt

In 2014, an American non-profit, One Green Planet, wrote about Aogashima in an article entitled "13 Amazing Natural Wonders You Should See Before You Die," making it famous worldwide. Since then there's been a steady stream of foreign and Japanese visitors. But the island is unequipped to handle many tourists. To get here from the mainland you have to first travel to Hachijojima, either by plane or by ten-hour ferry journey from Tokyo. From Hachijojima you take another ferry, or a helicopter that only seats nine, and for all this the cost is steep.

At the moment there are only a few places to lodge and they're aimed not at tourists but government employees and workers involved in civil engineering projects. On the day we arrived, we saw that the ferry passengers consisted, aside from our party, of only islanders, village officials and contractors. Our aim on this trip was to scout out tourist resources, and indeed there are some possibilities that can be pursued. But for the time being, the reality is that Aogashima will not soon become a tourist island.

By "tourists" we usually think of people who physically travel to a destination. But you could define tourists more broadly as the larger community of a place. For Japan, this means that tourism can aim not at merely increasing the numbers of visitors, but also at building up a community of people abroad who love Japan. In the same way that I love Schalansky's fifty islands, even if those Japan-lovers never visit, they'll carry Japan in their hearts. That by itself would fulfill some of the aims of tourism.

One of the best ways to build such a community is through the sale of local goods and foodstuffs. For example, I don't know if I will ever visit Parma, the source of Parmesan cheese, or Bordeaux, the home of Bordeaux wines, but for me these places have a special cachet. In short, a place can appeal not only through the flow of "people," but also through the appeal of its "things." With this in mind, we visited some of the locations on Aogashima where people are producing local goods.

We started at the western edge of Maruyama Hill where the volcanic steam, which the locals call *hingya*, rises from the ground. Nearby,

Hingya Salt

there's a pavilion where you can chat with the locals while boiling an egg with hingya steam. Beside this is a small one-room factory where they make Hingya Salt. The chief salt maker is Yamada Arisa, who was born and raised on Aogashima. In her younger years she was drawn to the theater, went off to Tokyo and worked as an actress in a drama troupe. When her mother got ill she returned to the island. Finding that no one was willing to make the traditional salt, she took this job upon herself and has dedicated herself to it.

Hingya Salt is made by drawing sea water into tubs and slowly evaporating the water by using the heat of the hingya steam. Inside the plant, the temperature is sauna-like, climbing to over 122 degrees Farenheit (50 degrees Centigrade), and twenty minutes is the longest that a person can stay inside. I came out after four minutes.

Because the sea water evaporates naturally and slowly, it forms large crystals with a slight sweetness. The taste is gentle, while also having the pungent flavor of sea salt. As the results of Yamada's efforts, Hingya Salt from Aogashima has gained a reputation among gourmet chefs in Tokyo and is in high demand.

Jungle leaves and shochu

Down the hill from the hingya steam fields is an area of dense jungle called Ikenosawa. There we were met by another young person who had formerly left Aogashima and since returned, Arai Satoshi who works as an island guide. In between managing his family's car repair shop and doing guiding work, Arai also practices as one of the members of the local drum group Aogashima Kanju Taiko (lit. "Aogashima Return Drums.") I thought the word "Return" a bit curious on first hearing it and only later learned its significance.

As we walked through the Ikenosawa Forest, guided by Arai, we observed around us the dense foliage of unfamiliar trees growing so thickly that they shut out the sky. You could feel that we were now in the tropics.

Arai drew our attention to a jungle plant with wide flaring leaves called *otani-watari*. A type of tropical fern, the Japanese name means "crossing the valley," presumably because the leaves are so long. These leaves are not just nice to look at. They serve a critical function in another local production, namely Aogashima's distinctive *shochu* (Japanese-style vodka). From Ikenosawa we proceeded to the shochu refinery.

The most famous shochu-making centers are in southern Kyushu, but shochu is produced all over Japan. It has a more lowbrow appeal than saké, and many well-known shochu brands come from islands like Iki and Okinawa. You can make shochu out of rice, but the islands have poor soil and undependable climate, and so rather than rice they use potatoes or wheat which are easier to grow and cheaper.

Another factor behind the excellence of island shochu might be the love of alcohol that we find in seaports all over the world. From fishing villages in Scotland to the city of Marseilles in the Mediterranean, people living by the sea love their drink.

Aogashima's shochu goes by the name of Aochu and has gained a following for its distinct flavor. There are about twenty different brands which vary according to the blend of potatoes and wheat, how long they're matured and the kind of yeast they use. There are ten people on Aogashima officially qualified as *toji* "brewers." With a total population of 170 people, this gives Aogashima by far the highest percentage of toji per capita in Japan.

On such a small island it doesn't make sense for each brewer to maintain their own plant, so everyone works together in one centralized brewery. Saké and shochu making are typically a male occupation, but in Aogashima it has traditionally been women who augment the family income by making shochu. So shochu brands are often given women's names (most unusual in Japan), of a mother or grandmother, such as Okuyama Naoko or Hiroe Junko.

What gives Aochu its special taste is the otani-watari leaves that we saw in the forest. The local tradition is to lay the long leaves one by one on top of braised wheat. The mold that then grows on the leaves mixes with the fermenting wheat, and from this is born a unique tropical flavor.

Brands of Aochu (Aogashima *shochu*)

The shochu of Aogashima and other Izu Islands has its roots in island exile. It goes back to a merchant Tanso Shoemon from Satsuma Fief in southern Kyushu. Shoemon was caught in Okinawa illegally trading with the Qing Empire and was punished by being banished to Hachijojima. In 1853, in order to conserve precious rice, it was decreed that people on Hachijojima could not use rice anymore to make shochu. In the meantime, the shogunate had been urging the islanders to plant more potatoes. A born entrepreneur, Shoemon saw his chance and introduced Satsuma-style potato shochu to Hachijojima.

Around this time, another man exiled to Hachijojima, Kondo Tomizo, was writing his history of the islands called *True Record of Hachijo*. The book gave a detailed description of the Izu and Ogasawara islands that is now seen as a critical source for knowledge of the archipelagos. He made special note of Shoemon's shochu, writing, "It brought great benefit to the farmers."

Potato and wheat shochu came, as the result of an exile punishment, from Satsuma to Hachijojima. From Hachijojima it traveled south to Aogashima where the locals infused it with the mold of the otani-watari leaves. And so Aochu was born.

The volcanic eruption of 1785

Aogashima has seen a slight decline in its population in recent years, but not enough to greatly affect the village. This is most unusual for a small island. It stands in strong contrast with all the other Izu islands—and with most villages in Japan—where populations are dropping calamitously. The two young people we met, Yamada Arisa the salt maker and Arai Satoshi the guide, had both left the island for a while, worked in the outside world and then chosen to return. One feels that the locals feel a deep attachment to their native place. Behind this lies the history of the volcano.

Lovely Maruyama Hill, with its striped forest cover, did not exist prior to the 1785 eruption. Before this, it's known now that Aogashima's volcano had erupted from time to time over several thousand years, but all that was long ago. Since the fifteenth century it had lain largely dormant, but it was still alive. There were two rumblings in the seventeenth century when the temperature rose in the lake that previously sat where Maruyama and the Ikenosawa Forest now are, and some volcanic ash was thrown into the air. It caused no great damage.

We can now see that these disturbances were precursors of the big one that was to come a century later. The magma was quietly building

Hingya volcanic steam rising from a hillside

up, and from 1780 the villagers started to feel a series of earthquakes. Finally, in March 1785, the volcano went into eruption and the lake vanished into a growing crater. Immediately several tens of houses near the center were destroyed.

The inner caldera, which is now Maruyama, began to grow from accretions of magma and scolia (volcanic debris). With their fields buried in ash, and lacking water, the villagers decided to flee to Hachijojima, but they couldn't just leave. Even today, villages in Japan depend heavily on local bureaucracies for many aspects of their existence. People can make few initiatives on their own. They must first deal with the town office, often located far away from their homes, where functionaries stamp documents to fund or defund, approve or cancel. In the Edo period, the restrictions were tighter, especially in the sensitive Izu Islands, directly ruled by the shogunate and a place of exile for criminals. To leave Aogashima, the villagers needed permission.

The island's headman Shichidayu sailed to Hachijojima with a group of people and there tried to negotiate with the local authorities for safe haven for the rest of the islanders. By the time approval came down, it was May, and when the three rescue boats reached the island it was already too late. With a volcanic eruption in full spate, the sky was pitch black even in daytime. Villagers crowded the dockside, many leaping into the water as they tried to escape the hot falling ash. The boats had to get away before the heat killed everyone, leaving old people and children to drown in front of their eyes. Altogether 140 people perished on that day.

The "Return"

About two hundred people escaped, including the group that Shichidayu had brought to Hachijojima in March. Now began many years of travail. The survivors had hardly escaped to a paradise. After several years of typhoons and failed harvests, Hachijojima was suffering from famines. According to the social hierarchy of the times, the refugees from Aogashima ranked even lower than exiled criminals. The two hundred survivors lived in absolute poverty.

Shichidayu, and the headmen that came after him, repeatedly sent boats to Aogashima with villagers hoping to reclaim their island, but the island was still a volcanic wasteland and a dozen tries ended in failure. Two of the headmen died at sea. After 1801 there were no more attempts, and Aogashima was completely abandoned.

But the villagers had not given up. In 1806 the headman of the time, Takichi, traveled up to Edo to request the shogunal authorities' approval for *okoshigaeshi* "resettling of deserted land." The officials said, "We'll think about it." Another decade passed.

In 1817 Sasaki Jirodayu took over as the new headman. By this time thirty years had passed since the eruption. Volcanic explosions had stopped and the island was sprouting new green foliage. In the meantime, the original refugees were aging, and their children and grandchildren, who had never seen Aogashima, made up the majority.

Faced with the danger that his village might disappear from the face of the earth, Jirodayu devoted the next twenty years of his life to the revival of Aogashima Island. He negotiated with the shogunal officials; he raised money; and he arranged for small groups to go to

The cliffs of Aogashima

the island and slowly build up canals, fields, pathways and the dock.

In 1822 the villagers started to return, and by 1824, two hundred people were living on Aogashima. In 1835, inspectors from the fief that administered the Izu Islands certified that the villagers would soon be able to pay taxes. With that, the rebirth of Aogashima village received the seal of approval from Edo. Historians argue about the date when the revival of Aogashima was finalized. The shogunal bureaucrats judged by taxes.

In the end it took fifty years for the okoshigaeshi resettling to finally be realized. In the 1930s, the great ethnologist Yanagida Kunio wrote a historical novel based on the tragedy of Aogashima called *Aogashima kanju-ki* [Record of the return to Aogashima], and since that time the villagers have used the word *kanju* ("return") rather than the older word, okoshigaeshi. Hence the Aogashima Return Drums.

But history is never quite what we think it was. In 2008, a researcher cast doubt on the whole story passed on by the villagers since the 1780s. He claimed that according to shogunal records that he had unearthed, there had been no tragedy, all the islanders had escaped safely.

However, one must keep in mind that these were reports dispatched to higher-ups in Edo by local officials who must admit no fault. One can't help but think of the recent history of the great Tohoku tsunami in 2011, when officials hid from residents of Iitate in Fukushima Prefecture the fact that their village was so seriously contaminated that it was unlivable. And hid for a long time from the world the fact that all three reactors at Fukushima had melted down. In the case of Aogashima, one can imagine how the reports got written. "No one has died on our watch. I would like to assure Your Excellency that volcanoes in our district are very well-behaved volcanoes." One therefore can't take documents like this at face value. It wouldn't be Japan's first or last bureaucratic cover-up.

Given the wealth of true-to-life details in the accounts handed down by the villagers, the body of evidence would seem to support their version of the story. Whatever really happened, the tale of the eruption is deeply burned into the memories of the people of Aogashima.

A hero of rural revival

In the 180 years that have passed since the *kanju* "return," it is remarkable that the island's population has hardly changed. The villagers' love for their island runs deep. But the volcano is still active, as we can see from the hingya steam rising from Maruyama Hill and Ikenosawa Forest. The people are living above a sleeping dragon.

In the Old Testament it's written that Moses led his people for forty years through the wilderness before finally the Israelites could settle in the promised land of Canaan. In *Aogashima kanju-ki*, Yanagida Kunio called the headman Jirodayu "the Moses of Aogashima."

In addition to the years in the wilderness, there's another parallel to Moses: the Ten Commandments. In researching Jirodayu's life, I was struck by the fact that when he brought the villagers back to their island, he made them all sign a Nine Item Pledge for Peace. He foresaw that Aogashima's greatest challenge would be internal discord.

The Nine Items proclaimed that all communal issues were to solved through peaceful cooperation. For example, the captains of the boats running between Hachijojima and Aogashima used to decide unilaterally whether a boat could sail or not—with the result that there were many fatal accidents. One of the Nine Items ordained that this decision could now be made only with the agreement of all the boat's crew—after which, it is said, such accidents ceased. Near the inn where we stayed, we found a monument dedicated to Jirodayu. Now that villages all over Japan are desperately trying to revive their declining fortunes, you could say that Jirodayu is a true Hero of Rural Revival.

With his Nine Item Pledge, Jirodayu was a visionary. When you look at the reality of rural revival projects nowadays, you always see opposition and complainers. Projects fail to achieve consensus, which makes the bureaucrats drag their feet, and things go from bad to worse. Ironically, there's another parallel to Moses, who descended from the mountain with his Ten Commandments only to find the Israelites worshipping the Golden Calf. Much the same thing happened in Aogashima. In 1828, when the villagers had all come back and the Return was well on its way to success, the island split into opposing

Sasaki Jirodayu, hero of the Aogashima "Return" (Photo: Aogashima City Office)

camps, and Jirodayu spent his last years trying to keep order between the factions. The Nine Item Pledge for Peace came to naught. It would seem that human discord is a law of the universe.

Our trip to Aogashima was only one night and two days, but we were deeply moved by this island where people live in the mouth of a volcano. On our last day, as we stood waiting for the helicopter to arrive at the heliport on the northernmost point of the island, I found myself thinking sadly, "Now we have to leave this place. I wonder if I will ever see it again?" I wish we'd had more time there. There are few places in Japan where I've felt such a strong pull.

The helicopter arrived in a whirlwind and swept us up into the sky. Looking back out the window I watched the cliffs as they slipped away into the distance.

10

Return to the Misaki Houses

Miura Peninsula, Kanagawa Prefecture

When I think about it, I realize that I've been seeking "Hidden Japan" for a long time, from my early days hitchhiking around Japan in the early 1970s, then finding Iya Valley, and in more recent years traveling for my work restoring old houses. But the roots go back even earlier, before all of that.

In 1964, my father, a US Navy lawyer, was posted to the American naval base at Yokosuka, on the Miura Peninsula, south of Tokyo. I was twelve years old at the time. From 1964–66 my family lived in US naval housing in Yokohama and I studied at an old Catholic school, St. Joseph's College, which had been there since the Meiji era, across the street from the Foreigner's Cemetery.

For my birthday in June of 1964, my father gave me a Minolta Autocord camera. Unlike the SLR (single lens reflex) cameras in use today which are wider than they are tall, the Autocord was vertical. It was a TLR (twin lens reflex) with two lenses.

You flipped open the top and looked down via a mirror through the upper lens, using that to set focus and aperture. When you pressed the button to take the photo, the shutter allowed light into the lower lens exposing the black-and-white film inside. The negatives were large, about 1½ inches (3 or 4 centimeters) square in my memory.

I adored this camera and used to take it with me on excursions around the Yokohama area. The fact that my family never worried about a twelve-year-old boy traveling on his own on trains over quite a wide area shows what a safe place Japan is.

To the north I went to the Soto Zen temple at Tsurumi, and on to Kawasaki Daishi Temple in Kawasaki and beyond, to Asakusa in Tokyo, and sometimes I made a day trip as far as Nikko. To the south I went to Odawara Castle, to the Tanabata festival in Hiratsuka, to Kamakura and elsewhere. My favorite destination was the little town of Misaki on the Miura Peninsula.

The American community of the Misaki Houses

In the early 1960s, the memory of the US Occupation of Japan, which had ended in 1952, was still fresh. Many foreigners who had arrived with the Occupation were still living in Japan, and a group of them established themselves in Misaki. In addition to businessmen such as Seymour Janow and Tom McVeigh, there were a band of veteran journalists. These included the photographer Horace Bristol, and Keyes Beech, who won a Pulitzer Prize for his covering of the Korean War. US Ambassador Edwin Reischauer and his wife Matsukata Haru were

Linda and Keyes Beech (Photo: Linda Beech)

a part of this circle. Keyes Beech, married to the effervescent Linda Beech from Honolulu, lived in a house in Hiroo in Tokyo.

Linda had studied Japanese in Hawaii when she was young, and after the war she came to Japan, taking a job in the GHQ (in the Daiichi Insurance Building) where General MacArthur ruled. She met Keyes, and the two got married. By this time it was the mid-1950s and tele-

vision sets were sweeping across Japan. With her blond hair and blue eyes, beautiful Linda, who spoke fluent Japanese, became a star on an English-teaching program called *Aoi Me no Tokyo Nikki* [Blue-eyed Tokyo diary].

A family watching Linda Beech on television (Photo: Linda Beech)

Linda was thus the mother of all the foreign *tarento* "TV talents" who have crowded the airwaves since. Such was her popularity that the story was told about the time she once found herself encircled in an anti-American demonstration. Sometimes these demonstrations turned violent, and at a similar incident some time earlier, a staffer at the US Embassy had had to be evacuated by helicopter. The crowd were shouting "Down with America!" "America get out of Japan!" when someone recognized Linda in their midst. The shouts switched to a great outcry, "Linda-san! Linda-san!" And then, after she'd left the scene, they went back to "Down with America!" MacArthur is quoted as saying, "More than the Occupation forces, it was Linda who brought peace to Japan."

My mother, who had grown up in Hawaii, was a childhood friend of Linda, and thus through Linda's introduction, our family got to know the rest of the Tokyo foreign community. Photographer Horace Bristol had built a complex of villas situated on top of the bluff overlooking the sea at Misaki, and the Janows, McVeighs and Beeches all owned or rented houses there. Our family would often visit Misaki at the invitation of one or the other of these families and stay in their houses for short vacations.

At Misaki, located on the southwest stretch of the Miura Peninsula, the cliffs are steep and the seashore is broken into many tiny bays and inlets. In those days, red pine trees grew along the slopes and at night you could hear the wind rustling through the branches. I photographed the pines with my Autocord, but I wish I had also recorded them. This was the sound—no longer heard today, with the loss of most red pines in Japan to a blight—of *matsukaze* "wind in the pines," famed in Japanese song and poetry.

Wind blowing through the pines at the Misaki Houses, 1965

Above the cliffs was a plateau where rice paddies and watermelon fields stretched away. In those days there were a lot of children belonging to the families at the villas known as the Misaki Houses. We used to love snorkeling around the rocks at the seashore below. Our parents gave us five yen for each *uni* sea urchin that we caught.

Syncretic Japanese and American design

Two things from the Misaki Houses have remained in my memory. One was that right next to Linda's house was a thatch-roofed farmhouse. I think this was the first time I became aware of thatched roofs, and of course I photographed it too. About ten years later I found and purchased my old thatched house Chiiori in Iya Valley. Since then I've had one long love affair with thatch. It all traces back to that farmhouse next to Linda's.

Horace Bristol was an accomplished architect. The Misaki Houses had a Japanese woody feel into which he imported American design. At Linda's house the central roof had big wooden beams and rafters

The thatched house next to Linda Beech's house

overhead like a thatched farmhouse, with wooden sliding doors and shoji separating the rooms, and at the same time a sunken living room of the type that was then popular in American ranch-style houses. The floor around the fireplace was lowered and people sat on sofas around this lowered space.

In other houses there was a fireplace with a ventilation chute above it and people drank their cocktails while sitting around that. Over forty years later, in the 2000s when I was designing my own houses for a restoration project on Ojika Island in Nagasaki Prefecture, I remembered those living rooms and ended up building a sunken living

The interior of one of the Misaki Houses

room in that same style of Japanese-American syncretism. It was so popular with visitors that I've gone on to design similar sunken living rooms in Iya Valley and at Chino in Nagano Prefecture.

I recently learned that Adrian Zecha, founder of the famed Aman Resorts, had also rented one of the Misaki Houses in the 1950s. As a young man in his early twenties, Zecha had gone to Japan as a journalist for *Time Magazine*, and so he too was a member of the group of expat journalists who frequented Misaki.

Zecha speaks fondly of his Misaki days and once told me, "The Misaki Houses are where I learned to love this country." Sure enough, when I look at Zecha's Aman resorts, I can see the indelible mark of the Misaki Houses. They were unique—maybe the first effort of their kind—in that they combined 1950s America with traditional Japan, featuring American openness and comfort, while using Japanese wooden beams and columns and sliding shoji doors. The villas exuded the happy *I Love Lucy* myth of that American era. At the same time, clinging to the pine-clad hills of Misaki, they were built with the materials and techniques of old Japan.

It was a happy discovery to learn that I wasn't alone in being inspired by the Misaki Houses when I did my old house restorations. Zecha took a similar approach in Bali and Thailand, and his Aman Resorts have gone on to exert an incalculable influence on world resort design. The seed for it all lay in Misaki.

Into the mists of memory

In 1966 my family returned to America, but from then on I would visit Japan from time to time for summer vacations. In 1972–73 I studied for a year at Keio University's International Center in Tokyo. Horace Bristol had left Japan, and many of the other members of the old foreign community had moved on. But the McVeighs and Linda still had their houses.

Seymour Janow had founded a technical consulting firm in Japan after World War II and had become quite wealthy. He owned a yacht which he kept at Seabornia Marina in Aburatsubo Bay, not far from the Misaki Houses. Seymour used to enjoy inviting friends down for an outing on the yacht. My naval-officer father had been fond of sailing and I'd grown up with him sailing around Florida and the Bahamas, so I knew how to handle a boat. Seymour hired me to come down to Aburatsubo and help on weekends.

By 1973, the Misaki Houses were in their fading years. I would sometimes go to visit Linda and would sit with her in the sunken living room drinking gin while she told hilarious stories about the old days. But meanwhile, I had discovered Iya Valley and I ended up spending most of my free time during my year at Keio far away from Tokyo, down in Iya.

I purchased Chiiori in the summer of 1973 with the help of a loan from one of the Misaki regulars, Tom McVeigh. That fall I returned to university in America and never visited Misaki again. Once or twice I thought of it, but Tom and Linda were long gone from Japan, their houses sold. While I had many warm memories, Misaki became a place in the distant past.

As I traveled around the country in my search for "Hidden Japan," I found myself remembering back to the Miura Peninsula. Going around the Yokohama area with that Minolta Autocord in my hands had been the beginning of my journey. Over the years the Autocord yielded to several generations of Nikons and Canons, and nowadays an iPhone. To this day I'm an inveterate shutterbug, snapping pictures of everything I see. I'm still doing now what I was doing sixty years ago.

As I get older, I've seen that Japan—and Asian countries in general—are different from Europe or many parts of America, in that the look of towns and countryside can change drastically in a short time. If often happens that I return to a place I visited just recently to find it utterly transformed. What remains is my photographs. I've come to realize the critical role that they play.

As I've written earlier, when I see a beautiful seacoast in Japan, I can't just sigh happily and say to myself, "Oh what lovely marine scenery." Instead, with a sense of dread, I wonder, "When will this scene be wiped out by concrete construction?" When I walk through an old town, instead of saying "What a charming street," I think, "When I come here again, what damage will they have done to this place?" Sorrow—a sort of sorrow in advance—clouds my vision. All I can do is photograph the beautiful—ephemeral—scene that I now see before my eyes.

The quest for Misaki after fifty years

We decided for our last search for "Hidden Japan" to try to seek out the Misaki Houses and the bay they overlooked. Departing from Kyoto, we took the bullet train to Yokohama, and rented a car, driving down the western Miura Peninsula coast, via Kamakura, Zushi and Hayama.

When our family had only just arrived in Japan in the summer of 1964, we went to stay in a grand house in Hayama. I remember looking out from the second floor and viewing Mount Fuji floating over Sagami Bay. This house is also where I saw my first tatami mats. I was hoping we could find this house, but while we drove up and down the Hayama road a few times, we saw no sign of it. I suppose it's no longer there.

Misaki fields, ca. 1965

A bigger problem would be how to find the Misaki Houses. I contacted Seymour Janow's daughter Merit, who's now a professor at Columbia, and she told me the nearest train station and the name of the little bay. We managed to drive near to it, but no matter how hard we looked at our maps, there was no sign of the bay or anything that reminded me of the houses. Giving up on maps, I decided to just follow my intuition. We took some back roads and found ourselves in what seemed to be the right neighborhood, with watermelon fields stretching all around us.

I have one strong memory of those fields. The foreign children of the Misaki Houses used to play along the paths that wound through the watermelon patches. Seeing hundreds of plump green fruits ripening under the summer sun, we thought, "No one will miss one watermelon," so we cut one out from a far corner in the fields and took it home with us. That evening the stern figure of a farmer darkened our door as he shouted, "Your children have stolen my watermelon. Give it back!" Of course it was too late to it give back, our parents had to pay off the angry farmer and we were roundly scolded.

Even now I think it's incredible that the farmer could have been aware of the loss of just one watermelon out of those huge fields of hundreds of melons. I can't figure out how he did it. But one thing remained with me, child though I was: in Japan they don't miss any details!

Finding the bay

We were now somewhere in the vicinity of the Misaki Houses, but the coast is chopped into numerous valleys and the roads along the cliffs would suddenly stop or circle back to their beginnings. Nothing looked quite right. I gave up, and thinking that at least we could get a good view of the ocean from a lighthouse we saw in the distance, we headed for that. But the steep road up to the lighthouse got narrower and narrower and finally our car could not proceed any further. Even turning around to drive back down would not be easy.

While we were stopped on the lighthouse road, a woman came up to the car and said, "We don't often see foreigners around here. You

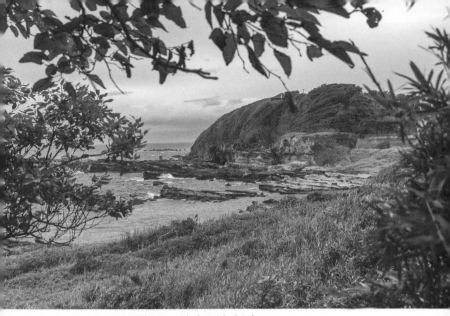

The coast below Linda's house

wouldn't, by any chance, be looking for the Misaki Houses, would you?" In shock, I murmured "Yes."

"Oh, this is so nostalgic," she said. "In the old days, my family used to look after the Misaki Houses. Ambassador Edwin Reischauer, Linda Beech and the presidents of Coca Cola and Hewlett Packard used to visit here." I mentioned that I had known Linda and she said, "Well, it's changed a lot, but I'll take you to where Linda's house used to be."

Without this chance encounter we would have driven around and around and never have found the Misaki Houses. We maneuvered our car back down the lighthouse road and she led us to a little path leading down to the beach.

Linda's house was gone without a trace, but I took one look and recognized the path we walked as children. I feel a sense of mystery and gratitude for the meeting with this woman because we could have wandered for days without finding this spot again. It makes me feel that even after the lapse of decades some sort of karmic bond still links me to this place.

Not only Linda's house, but all the houses built by Horace Bristol at Misaki have disappeared. Here and there new villas have sprouted up in the area, but they're the typical concrete-and-plastic boxes of modern Japan, a world away in feeling from the Misaki Houses. When we descended the path to the beach, however, nothing had changed. These were the same rocks where we used to catch *uni* sea urchins.

The rocks on the coast of the Miura Peninsula are striped white and black like the Susa Hornfels we saw on our trip to Hagi. However, there the resemblance ends, because unlike the smooth vertical Susa Hornfels, the rocks at Misaki are twisted and deformed from eons of volcanic surges and sea wear. They look almost like foaming waves.

As we walked along the beach, I remembered something else from childhood. It was the caves in the cliffs. In the closing months of World War II, the Japanese army dug in for a last-ditch defense of Japan's outer islands such as Okinawa and Iwojima in the Pacific. The islands were honeycombed with caves inside of which soldiers and civilians took refuge, only to die in the course of bitterly fought land campaigns. By the end of the war, the army was preparing for the same tragedy to unfold on the homeland. There were calls to the public to arm themselves with bamboo shields and spears, and to hide out in caves, hundreds of which were dug for the purpose. Sagami Bay and the Miura Peninsula had high military significance, so many caves were built on those coasts. Luckily Japan capitulated before those caves ever had to be used. In the 1960s our parents warned us, "Absolutely never go into the caves!" but driven by curiosity we climbed into those damp dark spaces more than once. I remember the fear I'd felt as a child, thinking "When war comes this is where we'll hide."

A dramatic inlet

From the beach near the Misaki Houses we drove to Seabornia Marina, where I was surprised to see that nothing had changed. The two-story clubhouse restaurant where Seymour Janow used to invite his guests was still there looking much as it always had. When we arrived it was already after closing time, but a kindly waiter let us in.

When I think about it, all the people I've talked about, my parents, Horace Bristol, Merit's parents Seymour and Selma Janow, Tom

McVeigh and his wife Maggie, Linda and Keyes Beech, they've all passed away. The number of people who remember the existence of that old American community are limited to a handful of old-timers such as me, Merit Janow and Adrian Zecha. I ordered a cup of coffee, and thought about the swift flow of human life and the changes I'd seen today. While the beach remained intact, the fields and new villas on the cliff above no longer had quite the charm I remember and had turned into the usual cluttered Japanese countryside. I had succeeded in finding the Misaki Houses, but so far we had not found the magical scenery which was our goal in all the journeys of *Hidden Japan*.

Thinking that if we drove further down the peninsula we might find an unspoiled spot, we set out on a quest.

At the southern edge of the peninsula is a small fishing village called Miyagawa-ko. At first it looked like the usual concrete-encased harbor, but we walked a way beyond the embankments, and found ourselves amongst a dramatic tableau of twisting Miura rocks. Here the mounds of rock rear up like huge frothing waves about to break. They spread farther inland and climb higher than they do at Misaki, extending for a long way down the beach.

That said, the sea beyond the beach was scattered with concrete blocks, and towering over the cliff behind it was a tall highway bridge. "There has to be an inlet somewhere that's still in its natural condition," I thought, and so we stubbornly pressed onward.

On this trip we were accompanied by Miura-born photographer Inomata Hiroshi, and he came to our rescue. He likes to go fishing along the coast and he'd learned of a secluded cove in another part of the peninsula. But he said, "It's going to be very hard to find if you're not from this area." And it was as he predicted.

After we'd winded over unpaved farm roads and through thickets, we found ourselves on top of a high rock face overlooking the ocean. Approaching the edge, we could see a terrifying drop over the cliff, but we couldn't quite see the total view. Finally, clinging to some tall grasses and a broken wooden fence, we could look down into the chasm where waves were clashing onto the rocks. The wind rustled

Inlet, Miura Peninsula

through the dense growth of stunted trees lining the cliffside just like the wind in the pine trees at Misaki. Behind us, coming right up to the lip of the ravine was the rich red soil of tilled fields, which made the sudden arrival at the precipice all the more unexpected. It was a glimpse of nature's wildness—something you rarely see in Japan.

We had found the last wild cove on the Miura Peninsula. But unlike other places in this book, its location will remain a mystery. It's not marked on any map. As we saw at the ancient shrine of Hiyoshi Taisha, old shrines and temples often have an *oku-no-in*, an "inner sanctuary" located far up a mountainside where few will venture. This place is my own private oku-no-in, the hidden sanctuary that only a handful of people know about. I hope it stays that way.

Postscript
A New Philosophy of Travel

I must apologize to my readers, since I haven't revealed the location of the Misaki Houses or the name of the wild inlet. To recap the words of Shirasu Masako quoted in the preface to this book, "When you find a place people don't know about, you want to tell them about it. But as soon as you tell them, it's immediately spoiled. Such is the cruel way of the world."

It was so even in her age, but today we face an unprecedented surge of over-tourism, which is impacting not only Japan but the whole world. All it takes is one good Instagram photo and tourists rush to the site. It might be the quietest hamlet or even a mountain peak; the crowds will appear. In May 2019, climbers on Mount Everest were caught in a traffic jam, with a line of hundreds of climbers perched on a precipitous ridge high in the sky. Five people died.

In March 2019, I published a book in Japanese called *Kanko bokoku-ron* [Destroying the nation with tourism], a riff on the recent government slogan "Build up the Nation with Tourism." I argued that while tourism is important to Japan, like any industry it needs good management or it produces toxic effects.

In Japan, the focus has been on increasing tourist numbers. There has been very little thought given to managing tourist sites once visitors arrive. And close to zero thought given to the ambience of the site's surroundings. Inside the manicured Zen temple, all is peaceful and perfectly pruned. Just outside the gate, chaos reigns. Or that's how it used to be. Nowadays the chaos is breaking through to the inside as well.

As chronicled in my book *Dogs and Demons* (2001), the econmy of Japan—and the incomes of bureaucrats—depends on never-ending civil engineering and construction works. This has given rise to the expression often used in Japan, the "construction state." In the construction state, agencies focus single-mindedly on building things, and they have huge budgets to do so.

I've long joked that no matter what the starting point—medical care, schools, sports or tourism—the end point is always the same, "Let's build something." Tourism thus brings the pouring of lots of cement, in the form of new and widened roads (with the embankments and mountain leveling that go along with them), big parking lots, construction of souvenir sales complexes and so on.

Handled with care, the construction might not be so bad. But Japan has no little to no scenic protection. This is true for cities, and especially true for the countryside. After the roads—or even before them—come concreted rivers, billboards, the cutting down of trees, leveling rice paddies with landfill, and shiny metal guard rails. Localities lack legal means to prevent the onslaught of junk and there's little interest on the part of the public.

Meanwhile tourism has made the authorities nervous of bad behavior. The energies of those in charge of famous landscapes, parks and temples go into installing bright signage warning against anything that could possibly go wrong. "Danger!" "Beware!" "No photos!" "No parking!" "No littering!" "Watch your step!" "Follow the route!" "No entry!" "Fire Prohibited!"—the signs go up haphazardly, often repeating the same message every few feet, piling up signpost upon signpost in the most scenic of places. It's a perfect storm. Tourism becomes an engine of destruction.

At the end of 2019, Japan was experiencing a boom in foreign tourism. Arrivals had shot up from 800,000 in 2010 to over 30 million in 2019. Projections were for 40 million for the Olympics, scheduled for 2020, and after that, onward and upward. Places like Kyoto, while pleased with the pluses brought by tourism, were also facing the minuses: sand gardens and idyllic paths swamped by chaotic throngs; overcrowded museums; clogged streets and sidewalks. Old shopping arcades which used to purvey fish and tofu to locals began selling matcha-flavored ice cream cones to tourists. The character of the city started to change.

In Kyoto, there have been cultural gains, for example, the renovation of *machiya* townhouses which might have been torn down. Starting in the mid-2000s, people began to restore machiya and rent them out to travelers as places for people to stay. This has saved well over a thousand machiya during the last decade.

But the machiya boom became the victim of its own success. As real estate values rose, the trend to save machiya reversed course. Rather than restore an old house, it's more cost-efficient to tear it down and build a little concrete block with a few rental rooms. By 2018 we were seeing a new wave of machiya destruction to feed a demand for mini-hotels.

The problems of over-tourism in Japan were being much discussed in 2019 and at that time people were starting to think of systems that would ameliorate it. For example, the village of Shirakawa-go in Gifu

Signage in Wakayama Prefecture. (Photo: Tony Wheeler)

Prefecture, famed for its *gassho-zukuri* thatched houses, had been grappling with unsustainable crowds in the fall season. The simple solution: the village set up an advance reservations policy for its fall light-up.

With regard to the clashing signage which has defaced so many temples and shrines, Nara's Todaiji Temple was one of the worst offenders, with signs in shiny bright lettering plastered on every one of its huge old wooden columns. And then, some time in mid-2019, Todaiji removed them all. Suddenly the temple was restored to its ancient grandeur.

Covid arrives

Japan experienced a lively dialogue about over-tourism in 2019. Then came Covid-19, which dealt a massive blow to tourism around the world and made cross-border travel difficult if not impossible from 2020 to 2022. In Japan, as in Italy, France and many other countries,

Covid arrives at Osaka Station

the travel industry was devastated. Faced with a collapse of income, the problems of over-tourism now became the last thing on people's minds. In Kyoto, the focus turned single-mindedly to getting people back. But of course the problems are still there. With Covid vanquished, or at least tamed, the pent-up need for travel all over the world is bringing about a new tourism explosion. The demand for travel to Japan will be huge, and the country will likely witness a boom like nothing before.

A new philosophy of tourism

The dilemma of modern travel is that visiting tourist sites, and even writing about them, can be damaging. And yet many rural towns and villages depend for their life's blood on tourist income.

As long as we live in an age where anyone can go anywhere any time, wonderful places will continue to be ruined. We stand at a revolutionary moment in the history of travel. Like it or not, we're being driven to a new philosophy of tourism. In the old days, we all (including myself for most my life) felt free to travel just about anywhere, as long as it was reasonably safe. Nowadays, we need to give some thought to how our trip can help, and not hurt, the destinations we visit.

Part of the answer will probably lie in slowing down. It's easy to see a lot in a short time and absorb almost nothing from it. But there's a way to travel which might be the equivalent of slow food versus fast food. When you stop to take in the details, time slows. Taking more time—sipping slowly—there's room for the spirit of the place to enter your heart. The damage you inflict decreases and the support you give to locations that need it increases.

As we saw at Amami in Chapter 6, with the "zero-dollar tourism" of visits of big cruise ships to a particular destination, high numbers of short-term visitors don't necessarily bring much benefit to the local residents. The typical Japanese bus tour also brings in close to zero dollars. A study done at one village popular with tourists found that the average visitor spent forty minutes. They took a photo, used the toilet, bought a 120-yen coke from the vending machine and left. Most of the income went to the bus company and Coca Cola. Meanwhile thousands of tourists thronging the village's lanes turned it into something almost unrecognizable.

Back in Iya Valley, thankfully our twisting mountain roads don't allow for big buses. Once you've arrived at one of our restored houses in a hamlet high on a mountainside, you spend the night. Our guests pay for the room, eat the local food or take a lesson in soba-noodle making, which supports the locals who live in the hamlet. The income from one Iya guest comes to dozens of times the income of a visitor at the "big bus village," that is, one overnight stay is worth a full busload—or two—of day trippers. And most of the money stays in the village.

"Tourism footprint"

Travel is two sided. As with the tea ceremony, there's the "host" and the "guest." The hosts are the temples, museums, hotels and other places that receive visitors. Most of the talk about how to manage tourism has focused on these. However, there are also the guests, who are us, the travelers. *We* need now to think before we travel, for example not flying on airplanes to reduce one's personal carbon footprint, a growing trend in Europe.

There's also what you could call your "tourism footprint." The impact of tourism is typically measured in money: how much income you fed into the local economy. There's no question that tourism brings many benefits, especially in Japan, where villages in remote places like Iya rely for their last hope on the income from outside visitors. But there's also a minus side to the ledger: how much garbage you've left behind, the degree to which you disturbed the life of the locals or altered the environment. Just as every car, airplane and air conditioner has its carbon footprint, every tourist junket has its tourism footprint.

The "new philosophy of tourism" will include a new category of travel destination. I don't think it has figured much in travel writing before now. It's "places not to go." Given the damage being done to fragile environments such as Mount Everest or threatened beaches in Southeast Asia, maybe the best thing we could do for the planet is to stay away.

After "places not to go," there's a second, bigger category, which is "places that don't need you." A key point of the new philosophy of tourism is travel as social responsibility. You can travel simply to have a fun vacation. Or you can travel as a way to help struggling communities and protect the environment—and have some fun along the way too.

In Japan, imagine that you're a traveler with limited time and resources and you're going to make some choices. You could go to the Golden Pavilion in Kyoto, which will be forever crowded, where your presence will make no difference whatsoever. Or you could go to Tashiro in Akita Prefecture, Wajima on the Noto Peninsula or the town of Hagi, which you can enjoy at your leisure, and where you would bring value to the locals. In other words, the Golden Pavilion is nice, but you needn't go. Other places will actually benefit from your visit.

Not only travelers, but writers have a responsibility. Our words and photographs also leave a tourism footprint, and sometimes it's a large one. It has been my pleasure for decades to write about the great places I've visited and describe their wonders for a wider world. In these days of over-tourism, I now stop and ask before writing: should I really introduce that quiet unknown temple in Kyoto or the wild inlet on the Miura Peninsula?

In 1688, the great haiku poet Matsuo Basho traveled around northern Japan, visiting areas that were seen as uncivilized and outlandish, far from the accepted beauty spots of his time. Basho wrote a poem-and-prose haiku journal as he went, later compiling his memories into a book called *The Narrow Road to the Deep North* which has become a travel classic. But *Narrow Road* was not really about travel. It was about the skill of appreciating small things—a waterfall that Basho watched in silence; his reverence for the clogs at the foot of a monk's statue. Of the famous Toshogu Shrine at Nikko, he gave almost no description at all, simply writing:

> Awe-inspiring,
> Green leaves, new leaves
> Shining in the sun.

Basho kept silent about the shrine buildings, and instead focused on the green leaves around them—and magically, in that process, he managed to conjure up the very essence of a shrine cocooned in its sacred grove. Meanwhile, "Shining in the sun" 日の光 cleverly uses the same Japanese kanji characters as the name Nikko, 日光, so the haiku is not just generically about green leaves—Nikko is there after all. In *Narrow Road*, Basho gave us a way of looking at things; it probably never entered his head that other people would later try to follow his footsteps.

Travel writers from centuries ago told us, "These are the marvelous places that exist in the world." They expected that their readers would let the descriptions expand in their hearts and minds—and leave it there. Judith Schalansky's book *A Pocket Atlas of Remote Islands: Fifty Islands I Have Not Visited and Never Will*, carried it even further. She only wrote, and never visited herself. My *Hidden Japan* was inspired by Shirasu Masako's *Kakurezato*. She never thought that her readers would follow after her. Her writing was to be enjoyed for the things she noticed.

I want to say to my readers, "Splendid locations like the ones in this book still exist in Japan." But you don't need to travel to them. Instead, look for something forgotten but wonderful in your own neighborhood. When you've found it, share it with a few close friends, and then keep it quietly to yourself.

Afterword by Kiyono Yumi

I n Alex Kerr's relationship with Japan, there were three defining moments.

The first came at the age of twelve. In a shop in Motomachi in Yokohama, he saw some old Imari dishes being unwrapped from the ropes in which they had been tied for a hundred years, and felt a sense of mystery and awe.

The second came in the 1970s when he hitchhiked around Japan. In the remote and depopulated area of Iya, he went inside an old thatched house and was struck at the *kurobikari* "shiny black" of the floors and beams.

The third came after he finished his university studies and found work in Japan. Looking for a place to live, he came across an abandoned dwelling in the grounds of a small Tenmangu shrine. Inside, it was a haunted house complete with spider webs. When he went to slide open the *amado* wooden doors facing the garden, the whole row of rotten old doors collapsed and into his eyes leapt a view of a green hillside with a stream below it and a sunlit mossy garden.

These stop-motion images were engraved in his memory and have guided him ever since in his devotion to Japanese culture. In his book *Lost Japan* [first published in Japanese in 1993, translated into English in 1996], he described living in a thatched house in Iya, and in the grounds of a Tenmangu shrine near Kyoto; as well as his experiences with calligraphy, Noh drama, and Kabuki. Energetically, he captured the essence of Japanese culture.

But as the title *Lost Japan* indicates, the "beautiful Japan" Alex had loved and sought out was already starting to disappear. Underlying each chapter there was a sorrowful sense of fragility and evanescence. That's the classic *mono-no-aware* ("sadness at the ephemeral nature of the world") that has been imparted into us by the delicate landscape of Japan that we live in.

Now, after fifty-six years have passed since he first came to Japan, he's written a book, which with the maturity of a lifetime, expresses that mono-no-aware all the more deeply.

As Alex wrote in the preface to this book, the Japanese tend to be more fascinated by the *ura* "back" than the *omote* "front," more by *mitsu* "hidden" than by *ken* "revealed." The tourist boom has been going on for a long time, and nowadays all it takes is one social media post for a place to be totally swamped. For that very reason, we long for what still remains "hidden."

The unconscious desire to explore the back and not the front, imbued with a sense of the impermanence of things, is at the heart of the journeys described in this book.

The travels in *Hidden Japan* ran for two years from 2017–19. The "Lost Japan" described so vividly when Alex was forty, has now receded further. With a sense of spiritual awakening, he leads his readers to another horizon. I feel these journeys reflect a truly matured sense of travel.

These chapters started as articles, first published in the quarterly magazine *Kotoba* and later the website *Shueisha Plus*. Throughout this time, we have benefited much from the support of Chiba Naoki of Shueisha's editorial department, for which I would like to express my deep gratitude.

Kiyono Yumi
Journalist, Editor and travel companion

Glossary of People, Terms and Places

ERAS IN JAPANESE HISTORY

Jomon	14,000 BCE–300 BCE
Asuka	538–710
Nara	710–794
Heian	794–1185
Kamakura	1185–1333
Muromachi	1333–1603
(Momoyama)	*(1573–1603)*
Edo	1603–1868
Meiji	1868–1912
Taisho	1912–1925

Abe Hisao 阿部久夫. Proprietor of bookstore and **Kakuzan** thatched-roof inn in the town of **Tashiro** in Akita Prefecture.

Aburatsubo Bay 油壺湾. A small bay on the west side of the **Miura Peninsula**, south of Yokohama, containing **Seabornia Marina**.

adan **plant** アダン. A hardy long-leafed plant that grows by beaches, *pandanus*.

Aibagawa stream 藍場川. A stream in **Hagi City** lined with old houses accessed via small stone bridges.

Aizu-Tajima 会津田島. **Tobu Line** station in **Minami-Aizu**, Fukushima Prefecture.

Aizu-Wakamatsu 会津若松. Castle town in the northern Aizu area, Fukushima Prefecture, scene of a tragic battle in 1868 between the imperial forces and Aizu-Wakamatsu's supporters of the shogunate.

akiya 空き家. Abandoned house.

Akiyoshidai 秋吉台. Grassy plateau in Yamaguchi Prefecture marked by countless limestone pinnacles. Designated a Quasi-National Park 国定公園.

ako tree アコウ (榕、赤榕). A semitropical tree with wide twisting branches, *ficus superba*.

amado 雨戸. Heavy wooden sliding doors along the outside of a house, usually left open, but closed when the owners are absent or during heavy wind or rain.

Amami 奄美. A semitropical island group, part of Kagoshima Prefecture, located between Kyushu and Okinawa. The two largest islands are the main island of Amami 奄美大島 and **Kakeroma**.

Aman. Name of a chain of upscale resorts founded by **Adrian Zecha**.

Ampo protests 安保条約. Protests running from 1959 to 1970, against Japan's defense treaty with America.

Anamizu 穴水町. Town on the west coast of the **Noto Peninsula**.

Ani-Nekko 阿仁根子. Secluded hamlet in Ani area of Akita Prefecture.

Aochu 青焼. Brand name of the *shochu* (Japanese-style vodka) from **Aogashima**, short for Aogashima Shochu 青ヶ島焼酎.

Aogashima 青ヶ島. Remote island in the **Izu Archipelago**, located 217 miles (350 km) southeast of Tokyo in the Pacific. Administered by the City of Tokyo.

Aogashima kanju-ki 青ヶ島還住記 [Record of the return to Aogashima], a book by ethnographer **Yanagida Kunio** (1933).

Aogashima Kanju Taiko 青ヶ島還住太鼓. "Aogashima Return Drums," a drum troupe on **Aogashima** Island.

Aoi Me no Tokyo Nikki 青い目の東京日記 [Blue-eyed Tokyo diary]. The TV program that made **Linda Beech** famous in Japan.

Arai Satoshi 荒井智史. Young nature guide on **Aogashima** Island.

Asakusa 浅草. Traditional neighborhood in northeast Tokyo, start of the **Tobu Line** to **Nikko** and **Minami-Aizu**.

Ashizu River 芦津川. Scenic river in the town of **Chizu**, Tottori Prefecture.

Azuchi Castle 安土城 (1579–1585). Built by **Oda Nobunaga**, it was the first great castle to have walled moats and a *tenshu* central tower. Famed for its lavishness, it was dismantled in 1585 by Hidetsugu, the son of **Toyotomi Hideyoshi**, after **Oda Nobunaga**'s death. Along with Hideyoshi's **Momoyama Castle**, it has given its name to the **Azuchi-Momoyama period**.

Azuchi-Momoyama period 安土桃山時代 (1573–1603). Usually shortened simply to **Momoyama period**. Thirty-year period of castle building and expansive, gorgeously decorated art, named after **Oda Nobunaga**'s **Azuchi Castle** and **Toyotomi Hideyoshi**'s **Momoyama Castle**.

bachigata 撥型. "Plectrum walls" which expand outward at the top, like the plectrum (*bachi*) used to strum a shamisen.

Basho see **Matsuo Basho**

Beech, Keyes (1913–1990). Pulitzer Prize–winning journalist who reported on the Korean War. Lived in Tokyo in the 1960s with his wife **Linda Beech**.

Beech, Linda (1925–2012). Charismatic Tokyo personality living in Tokyo in the 1960s, married to Keyes Beech. She was Japan's first foreign TV star.

Bigelow, William Sturgis (1850–1926). Wealthy Bostonian who traveled with **Ernest Fenollosa** and acted as patron for **Okakura Tenshin**. He built up a major collection of Japanese art, which he donated to the Museum of Fine Arts Boston.

Bizen ware 備前焼. Pottery made in the town of Imbe in Okayama Prefecture. Made from clay with high iron content, it's high-fired, but unglazed, having a strong reddish or purple texture, and sometimes dramatic flame marks from the kiln.

Boshin War 戊辰戦争 1868–69. War of revolution fought between the Edo shogunate and the supporters or Emperor Meiji aiming to restore the imperial family to power. It ended with the defeat of the shogunate.

Bristol, Horace (1908–1997). Photojournalist known as collaborator for Steinbeck's *Grapes of Wrath*, his reporting on World War II and his writings for *Life Magazine*. Based in Japan from the 1950s to the 1970s, he built the villas known as the **Misaki Houses** in the **Misaki** area on the southern **Miura Peninsula** south of Yokohama, where Tokyo expats such as **Seymour Janow** and **Keyes** and **Linda Beech** had homes.

buna ブナ (橅). Beech tree.

Burke, Mary Griggs (1916–2012). Major art collector, built up the largest collection of Japanese art outside of Japan, later donated to the Metropolitan Museum in New York and Minneapolis Museum of Art.

Butoh 舞踏. Originally called Ankoku Butoh (暗黒舞踏), an avant-garde dance form founded by **Hijikata Tatsumi** and **Ohno Kazuo** in the 1960s.

Byakko-tai 白虎隊. "White Tiger Unit," a group of 305 teenage samurai of the fief of Aizu at the time of the **Boshin War** in 1868 when the shogunate was overthrown by imperial troops. Nineteen of them committed suicide on a hill overlooking the castle.

Chiiki Okoshi Kyoryoku-tai 地域おこし協力隊. "Rural Revival Domestic Peace Corp," a program sponsored by the Japanese government to bring young people to live in rural towns.

Chiiori 篪庵. Name of Alex's three-hundred-year-old thatched house in **Iya**, Shikoku.

Chino 茅野市. A city in Nagano Prefecture where Alex restored four old houses.

Chizu 智頭町. A small town in the southwestern part of Tottori Prefecture, located inland, close to the border with Okayama Prefecture.

Cho'anji Temple 長安寺. Name of the original temple where **Ushi-to**, the Cow Monument now stands.

chona 手斧. Adze for cutting and smoothing wooden beams.

Choshu Fief 長州藩. A feudal territory covering what is now roughly Yamaguchi Prefecture, 1591–1868.

Colin Flinn. Young American working in Odate City in Akita Prefecture for the NGO Akita-Ken Tsurisumu "Akita Dog Tourism." Introduced Alex to the village of **Ani-Nekko**.

Daigoji 醍醐寺. A large temple complex in Yamashina to the east of Kyoto. The five-story pagoda, constructed in 951, is the oldest pagoda in Kyoto.

daimyo 大名. Samurai lords who headed regional fiefs, of which there were about three hundred.

daimyo gyoretsu 大名行列. "Daimyo parades"—entourages of lords traveling to and from Edo as part of their biannual *sankin kotai* attendance on the shogun.

Dairakudakan 大駱駝艦. A **Butoh** performance troupe ("Great Camel Battleship") founded by **Maro Akaji** in 1972 and still active.

Daishoin Temple 大照院. One of the **Mori clan** ancestral temples in **Hagi City**, Yamaguchi Prefecture.

deigo tree デイゴの木. A tropical tree with wide-spreading branches, commonly known as Tiger's Claw in English.

Dining Out. A culinary event sponsored by the company **One Story** since 2012, which aims to bring high-end cuisine to rural areas.

Dogs and Demons 犬と鬼. A book by Alex published in 2001 in both English and Japanese, on the subject of Japan's malaise since 1990. In particular it describes the mechanisms of Japan's addiction to public works projects.

dogu 土偶. Clay votive figures of gods and goddesses, made in the Jomon period (14,000–300 BCE).

doma 土間. Earthen-floored entry-room or kitchen area in a traditional house.

Edo 江戸. Name of the city (presently called Tokyo) that served as the capital under the reign of the Tokugawa shoguns. It is also used to refer of the period of their reign (1603–1868). After 1868, Emperor Meiji moved the imperial capital from Kyoto to Edo and changed the name to Tokyo, when it became the capital of modern Japan.

Edoya Yokocho 江戸屋横丁. Old neighborhood in **Hagi City**.

"Eight Views of Omi" 近江八景. A set of poems, often illustrated with paintings or drawings, describing scenic places near **Lake Biwa**. It was inspired by the set of Chinese poems "Eight Views of the Xiao and Xiang Rivers" (瀟湘八景).

Emperor Godaigo 後醍醐天皇 (1288–1339). Emperor with a life of dramatic ups and downs. Exiled to Oki Island in 1331, he escaped, raised an army and destroyed the Kamakura shogunate in 1333, only to be himself defeated in 1336 by Ashikaga Takauji, founder of the Muromachi shogunate.

Emperor Gomizuno-o 後水尾天皇(1596–1680). Emperor from 1611–1629, known for his achievements as an art lover and builder of temples and palaces.

Emperor Shomu 聖武天皇 (701–756). Emperor from 724–749 during the high point of the Nara period. He sponsored the building of **Todaiji** (Hall of the Great Buddha) in Nara. At his death, his widow donated his belongings to Todaiji, where they were stored in the **Shosoin Treasury**, remaining intact until today.

Enchin 円珍 (814–891). Fifth patriarch (868) of **Tendai** *Mikkyo* (Eṣoteric Buddhism) at **Enryakuji Temple** in Kyoto. He traveled to China from 853–858, returning with Chinese Buddhist treasures. Enchin founded **Miidera Temple**. After friction between his followers and those of the third patriarch **Ennin**, they descended the mountain and based themselves at Miidera, calling themselves *jimonha* "the temple faction."

Enku 円空 (1632–1695). Eccentric Buddhist sculptor based in the rural Gifu area who created works in a distinctive crude and abstract style.

Enma 閻魔王. Lord of the Underworld in Buddhism.

Ennin 円仁 (794–864). Third patriarch (854) of the **Tendai** sect of *Mikkyo* at **Enryakuji Temple** in Kyoto. He traveled to China from 838–847. Ennin's followers conflicted with those of **Enchin**, leading in 993 to a rupture in which the faction descended the mountain and based themselves at **Miidera Temple**. Ennin's followers remained at Enryakuji, and called themselves *sanmonha*, "the mountain faction."

En-no-gyoja 役小角、役行者 (634–701). Legendary mystic and magician.

Enryakuji Temple 延暦寺. A temple on the peak of **Mount Hiei** in northwest Kyoto. It is the head temple of the **Tendai** sect of *Mikkyo* (Esoteric Buddhism), founded by **Saicho** in 806.

Eshin 恵心僧都 (942–1017). Honorary name of Genshin 源信, a high abbot of the Heian era. He rebuilt **Cho'anji Temple** where the cow who worked on the project was later commemorated in the **Ushi-to** "Cow Monument."

Esoteric Buddhism see *Mikkyo*

"Evening Bell of Miidera" 三井晩鐘. One of the poems of the **"Eight Views of Omi."**

Fayan 法眼文益 (d. 958). Creator of a leading school of Chan (Chinese Zen Buddhism).

Fenollosa, Ernest (1853–1908). Bostonian who came to Japan in 1878, after which he was instrumental in saving traditional Japanese art. He was one of the founders of the Imperial Museum (now Tokyo National Museum), and teacher of **Okakura Tenshin**.

Forbidden Colors 禁色. Book with a homosexual theme by author **Mishima Yukio**, first published in installments 1951–53.

Foreigner's Cemetery 横浜外国人墓地. Old cemetery for the foreign community in Yokohama dating back to 1861.

Freer, Charles Lang (1854–1919). Industrialist and collector of Asian antiquities, who donated his collection to the Smithsonian Museum in 1906, and funded the building of the Freer Gallery of Art within the Smithsonian complex.

Fudo Myo-o 不動明王. Mystical Buddhist deity, protector of Buddhism, patron of ascetics and magicians. An image of Fudo Myo-o is enshrined within Seiryuji Temple in the town of **Yazu**.

Fujiwara Michinaga see **Michinaga**

fuki-urushi 拭き漆. "Polished lacquer," a technique of applying thin layers of lacquer to bring luster to pillars, beams and floors in traditional buildings in the **Noto Peninsula** area.

Fukuoka Fief 福岡藩. A feudal territory covering what is now roughly Fukuoka Prefecture in Kyushu, 1600–1868.

Furumachi 古町. A neighborhood of **Minami-Aizu** town where the Great Gingko tree is located.

Fushimi Castle 伏見城. Gorgeous castle (or series of castles) built by **Toyotomi Hideyoshi** in 1592 on Momoyama Hill, south of Kyoto, hence often called **Momoyama Castle**. After the first castle was damaged in an earthquake, Hideyoshi rebuilt a second castle nearby; and **Tokugawa Ieyasu** later replaced this with his own version. After being dismantled in 1619–23, parts of Fushimi Castle were donated to temples and castles around the country where they are still to be found.

gajumaru ガジュマル. Ficus microcarpa, a tropical banyan tree, found in **Amami** and Okinawa.

Gedatsu-mon 解脱門. "Gate of Liberation."

Genji 源氏. Military clan who fought the **Heike** clan for control of Japan from the mid-twelfth century, finally vanquishing the Heike in 1185. **Minamoto Yoritomo**, leader of the Genji, went on to found the Kamakura shogunate.

Genkaijima 玄界島. An island off the coast of Fukuoka, where criminals were exiled during the Edo period.

Genroku period 元禄年間. A Japanese era from the early Edo period, 1688–1704.

Gesshin 月心. "Heart of the Moon," the name granted to **William Sturgis Bigelow** on his initiation at **Homyo-in Temple** in **Miidera**.

Gion 祇園. Old geisha neighborhood in Kyoto.

gongen 権現. A term favored by **Tendai** Buddhism, it's the name used for Shinto gods who are avatars of Buddhist divinities or deified people.

Goto Archipelago 五島列島. A group of islands off the west coast of Nagasaki Prefecture in Kyushu.

Gyatei, gyatei 羯諦羯諦. Opening words of a sacred chant which ends the **Heart Sutra**, meaning "He has passed."

Hachijojima 八丈島. From the mainland coast, the seventh of the **Seven Islands of the Izu Archipelago**. It's one of the largest of the islands, located 174 miles (280 km) southeast of Tokyo. In Edo days many criminals were exiled here, including **Kondo Tomizo** and **Tanso Shoemon**.

Hachimangu 八幡宮. A type of shrine of which there are tens of thousands around Japan. Hachiman is a Shinto deity commonly referred to as the god of war.

Hagi City 萩市. Historic city in Yamaguchi prefecture on the Sea of Japan coast. It was capital of **Choshu Fief** 1591–1863, after which the capital was moved to **Yamaguchi City**.

haibutsu kishaku 廃仏毀釈. "Abolish the Buddha, Cast Out Shakyamuni" was the anti-Buddhist movement sponsored by the early Meiji state, 1868–1878. Thousands of temples were destroyed across Japan.

haikaraa ハイカラー. "High color," the word used in the Meiji and Taisho eras to describe sophisticated new Western imports such as coffee shops.

hakuashi 箔足. "Gold-leaf footprints," the patterns formed over time from slight impurities in gold leaf on old Japanese screens.

Hakuto Jinja Shrine 白兎神社. "Shrine of the White Rabbit." Its worship hall was donated to Seiryuji Temple in the town of **Yazu**, where it serves as a Buddhist sanctuary.

Hall, John Whitney (1916–1997). Professor of Japanese History at Yale University, author of *Village Japan* (1969).

han-akiya 半空き家. "Half-abandoned" houses (which are only visited occasionally by their owners).

hasa 稲架. Tall poles set up on the side of fields to dry the harvest, commonly seen in Akita prefecture in the north.

Hayama 葉山町. A town on the west coast of the **Miura Peninsula**, south of **Zushi City** and north of **Miura City**.

Hayashi Shinkan 林新館. Small inn-restaurant in **Chizu** town in Tottori Prefecture.

Heart Sutra 般若心経. Short, mystical Buddhist sutra, consisting of just 260 characters, recited by millions of people across Asia and the world daily.

Heike 平家. Military clan (also called Taira) who fought the **Genji** clan from the mid-twelfth century, finally defeated in 1185. Afterward, remnants fled into remote villages around Japan, among them **Iya** in **Shikoku**.

Hie Shrines 日枝神社. Name of a type of shrine related to **Hiyoshi** and **Sanno** shrines, all sharing an origin at **Hiyoshi Taisha**, which until 1868 was closely linked to **Tendai** Buddhism.

Higashi-Honganji 東本願寺. A large temple in Kyoto with massive columns made of *keyaki* (elm) wood.

Higashi Ushirobata 東後畑棚田. Rice terraces along the Sea of Japan coast in southern Yamaguchi Prefecture.

Hijikata Tatsumi 土方巽 (1928–1986). Founder, along with **Ohno Kazuo**, of the avant-garde dance style of **Butoh**.

hingya ひんぎゃ. Volcanic steam rising from under the earth on **Aogashima** Island.

Hinoemata 檜枝岐村. Village to the south of **Minami-Aizu**, in Fukushima Prefecture.

hinoki ヒノキ (檜). A type of cedar, used in construction and grown in industrial forest plantations across Japan.

Hiratsuka 平塚市. A city in Kanagawa Prefecture, located west of Kamakura on the Pacific coast. It's known for its colorful Tanabata festival in July in which large hanging decorations are strung up along the roadside.

hiwada-buki 檜皮葺き. Roofing made from many small cedar strips pressed together. It creates roofs with gently sloping lines, found in palaces, and also temples and shrines with high cachet.

Hiyoshi shrines 日吉系の神社. A type of shrine related to **Hie** and **Sanno** shrines, all sharing an origin at **Hiyoshi Taisha**. Until 1868 they were closely linked to **Tendai** Buddhism at **Mount Hiei**.

Hiyoshi Taisha 日吉大社. Located in **Otsu City**, at the foot of **Mount Hiei**, it's the mother shrine of the **Hiyoshi**, **Hie** and **Sanno** shrines. This and many others in this group have unusual *torii* gates with a triangular extension on the top.

Hiyoshi Toshogu 日吉東照宮. Located near **Hiyoshi Taisha**. It's the earliest example of the Toshogu shrines honoring the deified spirit of **Tokugawa Ieyasu**, founder of the Tokugawa shogunate. It was built in 1623 by **Tendai** abbot **Tenkai**.

hojo seibi 圃場整備. "Agricultural land redeployment," involving public works construction to rationalize, flatten and straighten rice paddies.

Homyo-in Temple 法明院. A sub-temple of **Miidera**, where stand the tombs of **Ernest Fenollosa**, **William Sturgis Bigelow**, **Machida Hisanari** and **James Haughton Woods**.

Honen-in 法然院. A temple on the **Tetsugaku-no-Michi** (Philosopher's Walk) in eastern Kyoto, known for its rustic thatched-roof gate.

Honji Suijaku 本地垂迹. "Original Essence, Dependent Traces." Doctrine of Buddhist primacy over Shinto which held that Buddhist divinities are essential beings in heaven, and Shinto gods are their descended local avatars on earth.

Horiuchi 堀内. Old neighborhood in **Hagi City**.

Horyuji 法隆寺. Temple located on the outskirts of Nara, the oldest wooden buildings in the world. The grounds include a five-story pagoda dating to the seventh century.

Hosoe Eiko 細江英公 (1933–). Japanese photographer who worked with **Mishima Yukio** and other cultural figures. He collaborated with **Hijikata Tatsumi** on the **Butoh**-inspired book *Kama Itachi* (1969).

hyottoko ひょっとこ. A comic mask used in folk performances, with a pinched mouth and twisted expression.

Ichikawa Beian 市河米庵 (1779–1858). A prominent Confucian scholar and calligrapher of the late Edo period, known for his crisp and refined style.

icho イチョウ (銀杏). Gingko tree

Iemitsu see **Tokugawa Iemitsu**

Ietsuna see **Tokugawa Ietsuna**

Ieyasu see **Tokugawa Ieyasu**

Iitate 飯舘村. A mountain village located northwest of the nuclear reactors in Fukushima Prefecture that were damaged during the 2011 earthquake. Radioactive substances drifted with the wind to Iitate where they created serious contamination.

Ikenosawa 池之沢. A forest on the island of **Aogashima**.

Iki 壱岐. An island off the northwest coast of Kyushu, between the mainland city of Fukuoka and Tsushima Island.

Imaizaki 今井崎. Peninsula at the northeast end of Amami Oshima Island.

Ingen 隠元隆琦 (1592–1673). Charismatic Chinese Chan (Zen) monk who came to Japan in 1654, and with the support of shogun **Ietsuna**, founded the **Obaku** Zen temple of **Mampukuji** in 1660.

Inomata Hiroshi 猪俣博史 (1968–). Photographer based on the **Miura Peninsula**, Kanagawa Prefecture, who guided Alex and his friends around Miura.

iraka no umi 甍の海. "Sea of roof tiles," an expression formerly used to describe the city of Kyoto when seen from a high place.

Iriki 入来町. Small historic town in Kagoshima Prefecture in southern Kyushu. The town's Iriki House is distinguished by a small vaulted thatched gate.

irori イロリ (囲炉裏). Floor hearth in an old Japanese house.

Ishitani-ke 石谷家住宅. Grand house in the town of **Chizu**, Tottori Prefecture.

Ishiyama-dera 石山寺. Temple in **Otsu City** to the east of Kyoto, founded in 747. Known for its rock formations and Japan's oldest extant *tahoto* pagoda.

Ise Grand Shrine 伊勢神宮. A complex of shrines dedicated to Amaterasu Omikami 天照大神, sun goddess and ancestress of the imperial line, in Ise, Mie Prefecture.

Issai Kyozo 一切経蔵. "Hall of All of the Sutras," a building housing a *rinzo* revolving repository of sutras.

Issey Miyake 三宅一生 (1938–2022). Leading fashion designer, famed for his pleated and wrinkled clothing.

Itaibara 板井原集落. A small hamlet located within the town of **Chizu**, Tottori Prefecture.

Iya 祖谷. A village in Tokushima Prefecture. Located in inner Shikoku, it's known for its steep mountains and thatched houses, one of which is Alex's house **Chiiori**.

Izu Archipelago 伊豆諸島. Long archipelago of dozens of islands stretching hundreds of miles south of the Izu Peninsula. All come under the jurisdiction of the City of Tokyo.

Izumo Shrine 出雲大社. One of the most important Shinto shrines, thought to be Japan's oldest, located in Shimane Prefecture on the west coast.

Izu Oshima 伊豆大島. Largest of the **Seven Islands of the Izu Archipelago**.

Janow, Merit (1958–). Daughter of Seymour Janow. As of 2021, Professor in the Practice of International Trade and Dean at Columbia University's School of International and Public Affairs.

Janow, Seymour (1913–2000). Co-founder and president of Tokyo-based U.S. Consultants Overseas Inc. from 1949 to 1981. Part of the expat circle based in Tokyo who had villas, known as the **Misaki Houses**, at **Misaki** in the 1960s.

Japan Pilgrimage ニッポン巡礼. *Nippon junrei*, the original Japanese version of *Hidden Japan* was published in December 2020.

Jigen-daishi 慈眼大師. Posthumous name of Abbot **Tenkai**.

Jigendo 慈眼堂. Temple near **Hiyoshi Taisha** Shrine, built in 1646 in honor of Abbot **Tenkai**.

jimonha 寺門派. "Temple faction," used to denote **Miidera Temple** and followers of Enchin who descended here from **Enryakuji Temple** after the schism with **Ennin**'s followers in 993.

Joeiji 常栄寺. Temple on the outskirts of **Yamaguchi City** dating from the fifteenth century. It has gardens created by fifteenth-century artist **Sesshu** and twentieth-century garden designer **Shigemori Mirei**.

Jomon period 縄文時代. Prehistoric period of Japanese history (14,000–300 BCE), known for its distinctive "cord-marked" pottery and *dogu* clay figurines.

Judenken 重伝建. Short for *Juyo Dentoteki Kenzobutsu-gun Hozon Chiku* 重要伝統的造物群保存地区, "Preservation District for a Group of Important Traditional Buildings."

juku 宿. Old inn town along one of Edo's major travel routes.

Kaga Fief 加賀藩. A feudal territory, 1595–1868, the largest of all feudal fiefs, covering what is now roughly Ishikawa Prefecture, including the **Noto Peninsula** and parts of Fukui and Toyama prefectures. Its capital was at **Kanazawa City**.

kago-no-ki カゴノキ(鹿子の木). Laurel.

kagura 神楽. Shrine dance.

kaiseki 懐石. Traditional haute cuisine, Kyoto-style.

Kakeroma Island 加計呂麻島. Long narrow island to the south of **Amami** Island.

kakurezato 隠れ里. "Hidden hamlets." Also the title of **Shirasu Masako's** book.

Kakuzan Inn かやぶき山荘 格山. A thatched-roof inn in the town of **Tashiro** in Akita Prefecture, run by bookstore proprietor **Abe Hisao** and his family.

Kama Itachi 鎌鼬 [Scythe Weasel]. A book by photographer **Hosoe Eiko** (1969) documenting **Butoh** dancer **Hijikata Tatsumi** in the Akita village of **Tashiro**. The word comes from a ghost story in which a mysterious scythe weasel, haunting the night hills, slices people before they even realize it.

Kameoka City 亀岡市. A small city bordering Kyoto to the west, home of Alex.

kamidana 神棚. A Shinto altar, usually small and located over head height, in a private home.

Kamigamo Shrine 上賀茂神社. One of Kyoto's oldest and most prestigious Shinto shrines.

Kami-Osawa 上大沢. A hamlet enclosed within *magaki* bamboo fences on the west coast of the **Noto Peninsula**. A few miles south of **Osawa** hamlet.

Kanakura 金蔵集落. A hamlet with a wide expanse of rice paddies, in the northern part of the **Noto Peninsula**, in **Machinomachi**, a village in **Wajima City**.

Kanazawa City 金沢市. A city in Ishikawa Prefecture, which was formerly the capital of **Kaga Fief**.

Kangaku-in 勧学院客殿. Reception hall of **Miidera Temple**, with *fusuma* sliding door paintings by **Kano Mitsunobu** (1600).

kanju 還住. "Return," the term used by ethnologist **Yanagida Kunio** to describe the return to the islanders in 1835 to the island of **Aogashima** after the volcanic eruption fifty years earlier.

Kanko bokoku-ron 観光亡国論 [Destroying the nation with tourism]. A book in Japanese by Alex (2018).

Kanko Rikkoku 観光立国. "Build Up the Nation with Tourism," a slogan pioneered by Prime Minister Koizumi (2001–2006) and used since to refer to Japan's new emphasis on encouraging foreign tourism.

Kannon 観音. Short for *Kanzeon Bosatsu* 観世音菩薩, the Bodhisattva of Compassion.

Kano Eitoku 狩野永徳 (1543–1590). Important painter of the late Muromachi era.

Kano Mitsunobu 狩野光信 (1565–1608). Painter of the late Muromachi and early Edo eras, son of **Kano Eitoku**, painted the *fusuma* sliding doors of the **Kangaku-in** reception hall of **Miidera Temple** (1600).

Kano school 狩野派. Lineage of painters, working in Chinese style with the addition of bright color and dynamic concepts. Preeminent in Japan since the later 1500s, the school was descended from Kano Masanobu 狩野 正信 (1434–1530) and lasted until the end of the nineteenth century.

Kansai 関西. "Western Japan," the Kyoto-Osaka-Nara-Kobe area.

Kanto 関東. "Eastern Japan," the area from Hakone up to Tokyo and beyond.

karayo 唐様. "Chinese style," a term used in traditional arts, in distinction to *wayo* 和洋 "Japanese style." Karayo tends to be grand, masculine, forceful, official, continental, delighting in the "glamor of nature": soaring peaks, luscious peonies, towering trees.

Kasari-wan 笠利湾. Bay on the north of **Amami** Island.

kashiwa カシワ(柏、槲、檞). Oak tree.

Katoku 嘉徳浜. A beach on the southwestern coast of **Amami** Island, threatened to be concreted over. Called "Jurassic Beach" by the locals.

kawaii 可愛い. "Cuteness," a sought-after quality in Japanese popular culture.

Kawasaki Daishi 川崎大師. A large **Shingon** temple in Kawasaki City, between Tokyo and Yokohama. Officially known as Heigenji 平間寺.

kayabuki no onami 茅葺きの大波. "Great billows of thatch," an expression used in contrast to *iraka no umi* 甍の海 ("Sea of roof tiles") in Kyoto.

Keio University 慶應義塾大学. Japan's oldest private university, founded in 1858.

ken 顕. "Revealed," used in contrast to *mitsu* 蜜 "secret." The term derives from Buddhist sects that teach the doctrine openly (*ken*), and those who pass them on esoterically (*mitsu*), with hidden knowledge divulged in steps to initiates.

Kenkyu era 建久年間. A Japanese era running from 1190–1199.

keyaki ケヤキ(欅). Zelkova, Japanese elm tree.

Kibitsu Shrine 吉備津神社. A shrine with elaborate roofs in Okayama Prefecture.

kitamae-bune 北前船. Merchant ships that sailed on a route that ran from Osaka through the Inland Sea, and up the Sea of Japan coast, via the **Noto Peninsula** and **Sado Island**. From there the ships continued along the western coast of **Tohoku** to Aomori, ending up at Hokkaido.

Kita-no-mandokoro 北政所 (d. 1624). Wife of supreme warlord in the late Muromachi era, **Toyotomi Hideyoshi**.

Kitano Tenmangu 北野天満宮. Head temple of the tens of thousands of Tenmangu shrines across Japan, devoted to Sugawara Michizane, patron god of scholarship.

koan 公案. An "impossible question" given as an aid to meditation to students of Zen to help them transcend rational categories.

Kogane-no-Oiwa 金大巖. The Great Golden Stone, enshrined at the **Oku-no-Miya** sanctuary of **Hiyoshi Taisha** Shrine.

Kokatsu Shuichi 小勝周一. A member of the Maesawa Scenic Protection Society 前沢景観保存会 in the thatched-roof village of **Maesawa** in **Minami-Aizu**.

Kokka Shinto 国家神道. "National Shinto," term used for the government organized and controlled nationalistic Shinto between early Meiji until the end of World War II (1868–1945).

komainu 狛犬. "Lion dogs," which vary and can be more lionlike or more doglike, often found in pairs at the entrance to temples and Shinto shrines.

Kondo Hall 金堂. "Golden Hall," the main hall of a temple; in particular, the main hall of **Miidera Temple**.

Kondo Marie 近藤麻理恵. Tidying-up guru, best-selling author and star of Netflix series released in 2019.

Kondo Tomizo 近藤富蔵 (1805–1887). Young heir to a wealthy family in Tokyo, he got involved in a land dispute in 1826 resulting in the murder of a family of seven. For this he was banished to **Hachijojima** Island where he lived most of the rest of his life. Author of *True Record of Hachijo*.

Koniya harbor 古仁屋. A small harbor on the south of **Amami** Island.

koyoju 広葉樹. Broadleaf deciduous trees.

kozai 古材. "Old wood," referring to beams, columns, etc., taken from dismantled old houses.

Kozushima 神津島. From the mainland coast, the fourth of the **Seven Islands of the Izu Archipelago**.

kuchiko クチコ (口子). Pressed and salted *namako* (sea cucumber) ovaries.

Kunozan Toshogu 久能山東照宮. Colorful shrine southwest of Shizuoka City, dedicated to Toshogu, the deified spirit of **Tokugawa Ieyasu**. Related in style to the main **Toshogu Shrine** in **Nikko**.

kurobikari 黒光り. "Black glistening," the shine on the smooth surface of old blackened wood.

Kuroshima 黒島. A preserved traditional town on the west of the **Noto Peninsula**.

kuyo 供養. A memorial service, or monument, for the dead.

kuyo-to 供養塔. A memorial monument, usually in the shape of a small pagoda.

Kyu-Yukawake Residence 旧湯川家屋敷. A preserved house open to the public in **Hagi City**.

Lake Biwa 琵琶湖. Japan's largest lake, located in Shiga Prefecture to the east of Kyoto.

Lost Japan. A book by Alex published in Japanese in 1993 under the title "Utsukushiki nihon no zanzo" 美しき日本の残像, and published in English as *Lost Japan* in 1996.

MacArthur, General Douglas (1880–1964). Supreme Commander of the American Forces in the Pacific, he oversaw the defeat of Japan during World War II, and from 1945–1951 headed the US Occupation government of Japan.

Machida Hisanari 町田久成 (1838–1897). First Director of the Tokyo National Museum, friend and mentor of **Ernest Fenollosa**, **William Sturgis Bigelow** and **Okakura Tenshin**, who introduced them to **Homyo-in Temple** in **Miidera**.

Machinomachi 町野町. A township in **Wajima City** on the north shore of the **Noto Peninsula**, location of the **Kanakura** rice terraces.

Maebashi City 前橋市. A city in Gunma Prefecture, north of Tokyo.

Maesawa hamlet 前沢集落. A hamlet of *magariya* (L-shaped thatched houses) in the town of **Minami-Aizu**, Fukushima Prefecture.

magaki 間垣. A tall fence made of bamboo rushes, set up around seaside villages in remote areas along the Sea of Japan coast.

magariya 曲り家. L-shaped thatched houses prevalent in **Tohoku** (northern Japan).

makara マカラ (摩伽羅、摩竭魚). A mythical sea monster, often appearing on roof flares or gate-beams of temples and shrines.

Mampukuji Temple 萬福寺. Head temple of the **Obaku** Zen sect, founded in 1660 by Chinese abbot **Ingen**.

Maro Akaji 麿赤兒 (1943–). Founder and director of **Butoh** troupe **Dairakudakan**.

Maruyama 丸山. Low mountain in the center of **Aogashima** Island, which is the innermost of double volcanic cones.

matsu マツ(松). Japanese red pine, now largely wiped out due to an insect blight that swept Japan after 1946.

matsukaze 松風. "Wind in the pines," an expression in traditional poetry.

Matsuo Basho 松尾芭蕉 (1644–1694). Japan's greatest haiku poet, author of the haiku-travelogue *The Narrow Road to the Deep North*.

McVeigh, Tom. American businessman living in Tokyo in the 1960s, a member of the expat community who had villas at **Misaki** known as the **Misaki Houses**.

Meiji Restoration 明治維新. 1868 revolution, led by the young Emperor Meiji (1852–1912; reigned 1867–1912) which overthrew the 250-year-old Edo shogunate and restored the imperial house to power.

Michinaga 藤原道長 (966–1028). Fujiwara Michinaga, powerful imperial regent in Kyoto at the high point of the **Heian** era.

Michi-no-Eki 道の駅. "Roadside Station" multi-purpose facility with parking lots, shops and restaurants, set up by the government at tourist sites throughout Japan.

Miidera Temple 三井寺. Important center of **Tendai Mikkyo** (Esoteric Buddhism), located in **Otsu City** just to the east of Kyoto.

Mikkyo 密教. Literally "Hidden teachings," usually translated as Esoteric Buddhism. Rich in mystical chants and complex iconography, it's related to Tibetan Buddhism. The two main sects of Mikkyo in Japan are **Shingon**, based at **Mount Koya** south of Nara; and **Tendai**, based at **Enryakuji Temple** in northeast Kyoto.

Mikurajima 御蔵島. From the mainland coast, the sixth of the **Seven Islands of the Izu Archipelago**.

Minami-Aizu 南会津町. A town located in rural Fukushima Prefecture.

Minamoto Yoritomo 源頼朝 (1147–1199). **Genji** clan warrior who defeated the **Heike** clan and founded the Kamakura shogunate in 1185.

Ming dynasty 明朝. Chinese dynasty 1368–1644.

minka 民家. An old Japanese house, sometimes called *kominka* "old house" 古民家.

Misaki 三崎町. A part of **Miura City** located on the southwest of the **Miura Peninsula** (south of Yokohama).

Misaki Houses. A group of villas in **Misaki** designed by **Horace Bristol** and rented or sold to American expats resident in the Tokyo–Yokohama area in the 1950s–1970s.

Mishima Yukio 三島由紀夫 (1925–1970). Controversial novelist, author of many best-selling books including his first novel *Forbidden Colors*, with a homosexual story.

Mitaki-en みたき園. A natural foods restaurant located in the forest in northeastern **Chizu** town in Tottori Prefecture, managed by **Teratani Setsuko**.

mitsu 蜜. "Secret," used in contrast to *ken* 顕 "revealed." The term derives from Buddhist sects that teach the doctrine openly (*ken*), and those who pass them on esoterically (*mitsu*), with hidden knowledge divulged in steps to initiates. *Mitsu* is the root of the word *Mikkyo* (Esoteric Buddhism).

Miura City 三浦市. A city at the southern end of the **Miura Peninsula**, containing the **Misaki** township area.

Miura Peninsula 三浦半島. A peninsula south of Yokohama. On the northwest coast is the historic town of Kamakura; on the east coast the big naval base of Yokosuka; to the south is the area of **Misaki**.

miyabi 雅. "Elegance," a word used to describe the courtly elegance of old Kyoto.

Miyagawa-ko 宮川港. A small fishing harbor on the southern coast of the **Miura Peninsula**.

Miyakejima 三宅島. From the mainland coast, the fifth of the **Seven Islands of the Izu Archipelago**.

Miyazaki 宮崎市. A city on the east coast of southern Kyushu.

Mokuan 木庵性瑫 (1611–1684). A disciple of **Obaku** Zen founder, Chinese monk **Ingen**. He came to Japan with Ingen from China, and became the Second Abbot of **Mampukuji Temple.**

Momoyama Castle 桃山城 (1592–1623). Informal name of **Toyotomi Hideyoshi's** two **Fushimi** castles, taken from the name of the hill (Momoyama, "Peach Mountain"), where peach trees (*momo*) used to grow. Along with **Oda Nobunaga's Azuchi Castle**, it has given its name to the **Azuchi-Momoyama** period.

Momoyama period 桃山時代. Officially called the **Azuchi-Momoyama** period it spanned the last decades of the Muromachi era, 1573–1603. It's noted for the wealth and glamor of the art and architecture created by **Oda Nobunaga** and **Toyotomi Hideyoshi**, powerful military rulers of the time.

Mori clan 毛利家. Hereditary lords of **Choshu Fief**, of which **Hagi City** was the capital until the late Edo period (1863), after which the capital was at **Yamaguchi City** (1863–1868).

Mori Terumoto 毛利輝元 (1553–1625). Founding lord of **Choshu Fief** in the early Edo period.

Morikawa Jinkuro 森川仁久郎. Proprietor of a *namako* marine-produce business in the fishing village of **Nakai-minami**, in the township of **Anamizu** 穴水町, on the eastern shore of the **Noto Peninsula**.

Morikawa Yasuko 森川康子. Wife of **Morikawa Jinkuro**.

Motomachi 元町. A historic shopping street in Yokohama.

Motonosumi Shrine 元乃隅稲成神社. A shrine in Yamaguchi Prefecture, noted for its dozens of red *torii* gates leading down the mountainside.

Mount Daisen 大仙. A mountain in western Tottori Prefecture.

Mount Hiei 比叡山. Guardian mountain of Kyoto, standing to the northeast in the "unlucky direction." On its peak is **Enryakuji**, head temple of **Tendai** Buddhism.

Mount Koya 高野山. Large complex of temples in the mountains south of Nara, center of **Shingon** Esoteric Buddhism. Also referred to as Koya-san.

Muroji Temple 室生寺. Ancient temple in the mountains of Nara Prefecture, noted for its charming small-scale five-story pagoda, built 800.

Nagato City 長門市. A city in Yamaguchi Prefecture bordering the Sea of Japan, south of **Hagi City**.

Nagato-no-kuni 長門国. The old feudal fief comprising the western (seaward) half of what is now Yamaguchi Prefecture. In the early seventeenth century, it merged with **Suo-no-kuni** to become **Choshu Fief**.

Nakai-minami 中居南. A small fishing port in the town of **Anamizu** 穴水町, on the east coast of the **Noto Peninsula**.

namako ナマコ（海鼠）. Sea cucumber

Nansenji Temple 南泉寺. A small temple in **Minami-Aizu** town, with a charming thatched gate.

Nanzanso 南山荘. A historic *magariya* house in Minami-Aizu which is used for special events.

Narrow Road to the Deep North 奥の細道. A travelogue by famed haiku poet **Matsuo Basho** (1702), describing his trip up to northern **Tohoku**.

Nase 名瀬. A port on the northwest coast of **Amami** Island.

Niijima 新島. From the mainland coast, the third of the **Seven Islands of the Izu Archipelago**.

Nijo Palace 二条城. Castle-palace built at the beginning of the Edo shogunate by **Tokugawa Ieyasu** (1603). Known for its gorgeous *fusuma* sliding doors and wall paintings.

Nikko 日光. Town in Tochigi Prefecture north of Tokyo, in which is located the lavishly decorated **Toshogu Shrine**, dedicated to the deified spirit of **Tokugawa Ieyasu**.

Ninnaji Temple 仁和寺. Major temple complex in Kyoto, with a *rinzo* revolving sutra container.

Nishiho Kaigan 西保海岸. Cliffs on the northwest shore of the **Noto Peninsula**.

Nishikomi 西古見. Small port on the southwest of **Amami** Island.

Noto Peninsula 能登半島. Part of Ishikawa Prefecture, a long peninsula extending into the Sea of Japan to the northeast of **Kanazawa City**.

Nuuanu Pali Lookout. Viewing spot on Oahu Island, Hawaii, overlooking spectacular cliffs.

Obaku 黄檗宗. One of Japan's three major sects of Zen Buddhism, founded in 1660 by Chinese Chan (Zen) abbot **Ingen**. The head temple is **Mampukuji** located south of Kyoto.

ochiudo 落人. "Refugees," usually on the losing side of a war. The term usually refers to the refugees from the **Genji-Heike** wars of the late twelfth century.

Oda Nobunaga 織田信長 (1534–1582). First of the three great warlords of the late sixteenth century, Nobunaga unified Japan after a century of domestic warfare. He was succeeded as ruler of Japan by **Toyotomi Hideyoshi**, and later **Tokugawa Ieyasu**.

Odate City 大館市. City in northern Akita Prefecture.

Odawara Castle 小田原城. Castle located in Odawara City, in Kanagawa Prefecture, west of the **Miura Peninsula**.

Ogasawara Islands 小笠原諸島. A remote group of tropical islands located 620 miles (1,000 km) south of Tokyo, but under the jurisdiction of the City of Tokyo, along with the **Izu Archipelago** islands which are closer to the mainland.

Ohno Kazuo 大野一雄 (1906–2010). One of the co-founders of **Butoh** avant-garde dance, along with **Hijikata Tatsumi**.

Ohno Yoshito 大野慶人 (1938–2020). Son of **Ohno Kazuo** who performed as a boy with **Hijikata Tatsumi** at the seminar performance of **Butoh** in 1959.

Ojika Island 小値賀島. Island at the north of the Goto Peninsula, off the western coast of Nagasaki Prefecture where Alex restored a group of old houses.

Okakura Tenshin 岡倉天心 (1863–1913). Disciple of **Ernest Fenollosa** who traveled around Japan with Fenollosa studying Japanese art. Following Fenollosa's term as curator of Asian art at the Boston Museum of Fine Arts, Tenshin became the next curator. Author of widely read book (written in English) *The Book of Tea*.

okami 女将. "Madame" of an inn or restaurant.

Okinoshima Island 隠岐島. An island, actually a group of islands, located in the Sea of Japan, belonging to Shimane Prefecture. They're famous as being the place where nobles and emperors, notably **Emperor Godaigo** in the early fourteenth century, were sent into exile.

okoshigaeshi 起返. "Resettling," the name used in Edo days for the villagers return to **Aogashima**, replaced in the early twentieth century with the word *kanju* ("return").

oku-no-in 奥の院. "Inner hall," which could also be the outermost sanctum of a temple complex.

Oku-no-Miya 奥宮. The inner sanctuary of **Hiyoshi Taisha** Shrine. Also used as a general term for the "inner shrine" or the outermost sanctum of a shrine complex.

Omomo-no-butai 大桃の舞台. A small rustic stage in the hamlet of Omomo in the southern part of **Minami-Aizu** town.

omote 表. "The front," that is, well-known and easily accessible places or ideas. Used in contrast to *ura*, "the back," things which are hidden and esoteric.

omotenashi おもてなし. "Hospitality."

One Story. A company associated with PR firm Hakuhodo, which since 2012 has arranged the **Dining Out** culinary events in rural areas across Japan.

Onin War 応仁の乱. The war which started in Kyoto 1467–77, leading to a century of devastating warfare across Japan.

Ono-no-Komachi 小野小町. (ca. 825–900) Legendary beauty and poetess of the Heian era.

Osawa 大沢. A hamlet on the western shore of the **Noto Peninsula**, surrounded by *magaki* bamboo fences. A few miles north of **Kami-Osawa** hamlet.

Oshima Strait 大島海峡. Ocean strait between the islands of **Amami** and **Kakeroma**.

oshoya 大庄屋. "Great Headman," powerful head of a town or village in Edo days.

otani-watari オオタニワタリ(大谷渡). A type of fern (called bird's nest fern in English) with long broad leaves, used in the process of making *shochu* liquor on the island of **Aogashima**.

Otsu City 大津市. Town on the southern shore of **Lake Biwa**, just to the east of Kyoto.

Ouchi clan 大内氏. Powerful lords who ruled the area of Yamaguchi from the fourteenth to the late sixteenth centuries.

Ouchi-juku 大内宿. Preserved inn town with old thatched houses, in **Minami-Aizu** county, Fukushima Prefecture.

Ou-saka 逢坂. The old road between **Lake Biwa** and Kyoto.

Owari Fief 尾張藩. Feudal fief (1610–1868), governed by a branch of the Tokugawa shogunal family, roughly corresponding to modern-day Nagoya and its environs.

pailou 牌樓. A kind of Chinese ceremonial gate with open columns and elaborate roofs.

Philosophers' Walk see **Tetsugaku-no-Michi**

Price, Etsuko and **Joe (1929–)**. Major collectors of Japanese art, who donated a number of pieces to the Los Angeles County Museum of Art, and sold the body of the collection to the Idemitsu Museum in Tokyo in 2020.

Qing dynasty 清朝. Chinese dynasty from 1644–1912.

Qufu 曲阜. Hometown of Confucius (551–479 BCE) and site of an extensive palace where the descendants of Confucius lived. Located on the Shandong Peninsula in northern China.

ranma 欄間. Lintels placed in the overhead spaces between rooms in old houses, often with elaborate carvings or latticework.

Reischauer, Edwin (1910–1990). Scholar of Asian studies, US Ambassador to Japan (1961–1965). His wife was Matsukata Haru (1915–1998).

Rinzai Zen 臨済宗. One of Japan's three leading Zen sects, with important temples based in Kyoto such as Myoshinji, Nanzenji and Daitokuji.

rinzo 輪蔵. "Revolving repository," a tall hexagonal container for Buddhist sutras which revolves when pushed, spreading Buddhist merit into the world.

Rurikoji Temple 瑠璃光寺. Temple in **Yamaguchi City** built by the **Ouchi clan**, with an important five story pagoda (1442).

sabi see *wabi* and *sabi*

Sado Island 佐渡ヶ島. Large butterfly-shaped island in the Sea of Japan, belonging to Niigata Prefecture. The shogunal gold mines were located here and it was a place of exile for mine laborers as well as for emperors and court nobles.

Saicho 最澄 (766–822). Monk who visited China 804–805 where he studied **Tendai** (Chinese Tiantai) Esoteric Buddhism, which he brought back to Japan. He founded the temple of **Enryakuji** on the peak of **Mount Hiei** in northwest Kyoto in 806.

Saikoku Sanjusansho 西国三十三所. Ancient pilgrimage route "Thirty-three Temples of Western Japan," established since the twelfth century. Dedicated to the goddess of compassion, **Kannon**.

Sakamoto Inn 湯宿さか本. Traditional inn on the north shore of the **Noto Peninsula** in **Suzu City**, known for its natural ambience and food cooked by gourmet chef and owner **Sakamoto Shin'ichiro**.

Sakamoto, Michael (1967–). Japanese-American scholar, performer of **Butoh** avant-garde dance and photographer.

Sakamoto Shin'ichiro 坂本新一郎. Proprietor and chef at the **Sakamoto Inn** in **Suzu City** on the north shore of the **Noto Peninsula**.

sakura サクラ(桜). Cherry tree.

Sanchayagai 三茶屋街. Preserved traditional neighborhood in **Kanazawa City,** Ishikawa Prefecture.

sando 参道. Path of approach to a temple or shrine complex, or to a sanctuary within such a complex.

Saneku Beach 実久浜. Beach at the western end of **Kakeroma** Island in the **Amami** group.

Sankaijuku 山海塾. A leading **Butoh** dance group founded in 1975 by Amagatsu Ushio 天児牛大 (1949–).

sanmon 三門、山門. Main gate to a temple complex. In the case of **Enryakuji Temple,** it refers to the "mountain gate," i.e., the main temple on the peak of **Mount Hiei.**

sanmonha 山門派. "Mountain faction" used in contrast to the *jimonha* "Temple faction" of **Tendai** Buddhism. The sanmonha descended from the followers of **Ennin** who stayed at **Enryakuji Temple,** after the followers of **Enchin** descended to **Miidera Temple** in 993.

Sannomiya 三宮. One of the pair of buildings, along with **Ushio-gu,** at the **Oku-no-Miya** inner sanctuary of **Hiyoshi Taisha** Shrine.

Sanno shrines 山王神社. A type of Shinto shrine found across the country related to **Hiyoshi Taisha.**

sanrin-o 山林王. "Forestry baron."

Sasaki Jirodayu 佐々木次郎太夫. Headman of the **Aogashima** Island villagers after 1817, who led the return to **Aogashima,** completed in 1835.

Sasanami-ichi 佐々並市. A small preserved village on the outskirts of **Hagi City.**

Sato Tetsuya 佐藤哲也. Village head of **Ani-Nekko,** in northern Akita Prefecture.

Satori-no-Michi 悟りの道. "Enlightenment Walk" linking temples and shrines on the hillside above the fishing port of **Nakai-minami,** located on the east coast of the **Noto Peninsula.**

Satsuma Fief 薩摩藩. Feudal fief roughly covering what is now Kagoshima Prefecture in southern Kyushu. The lords of Satsuma conquered the southern islands including **Amami** and others all the way down to the Kingdom of Ryukyu (Okinawa).

Schalansky, Judith (1980–). German writer, book designer and publisher, author of the book *A Pocket Atlas of Remote Islands.*

Seabornia Marina リビエラシーボニアマリーナ. Yacht harbor in **Aburatsubo Bay** in **Misaki** on the **Miura Peninsula. Seymour Janow** used to keep his yacht here.

Seiryoji Temple 清凉寺. A Jodo (Pure Land Buddhist) temple in northwest Kyoto, with a revolving *rinzo* scripture repository.

Seitokuji Temple 清徳寺. A **Shingon** temple in the town of **Yazu,** Tottori Prefecture, known for its ancient trees.

Sekidera 関寺. An ancient temple on the **Ou-saka** road between **Lake Biwa** and Kyoto, now the site of **Cho'anji Temple.** The **Ushi-to** "Cow Monument" stands in the grounds.

Sekigahara 関ヶ原. Major battle fought in October 1600 in which **Tokugawa Ieyasu** defeated his enemies, leading to the founding of the Edo shogunate.

sekishu-gawara 石州瓦. "Sekishu tiles," made in Shimane Prefecture, known for their distinctive orange-maroon color.

Sesshin 雪心. "Heart of Snow," the name granted to **Okakura Tenshin** on his initiation at **Homyo-in Temple** in **Miidera**.

Sesshu 雪舟 (1420–1506). Greatest painter of the Muromachi era, founder of the Unkoku School of ink painting; also known for his garden designs.

Seto Kunikatsu 瀬戸國勝. Modernistic lacquer artist of **Wajima, Noto Peninsula**.

Setouchi 瀬戸内町. A town covering the southern part of **Amami** Island.

Seven Islands of the Izu Archipelago 伊豆七島. Of the many islands of the Izu archipelago, these are considered the most important. From the closest to the mainland coast, they are: **Izu Oshima, Toshima, Niijima, Kozushima, Miyakejima, Mikurajima and Hachijojima.**

Shakemachi 社家町. A neighborhood near **Kamigamo Shrine** in Kyoto, formerly lived in by shrine priests (*shake* 社家). Houses stand along a small stream and are entered by stone bridges over the stream.

Shichidayu 七太夫. The headman of the **Aogashima** Island villagers at the time of the volcano eruption in 1785.

Shigemori Mirei 重森 三玲 (1896–1975). Prominent Japanese garden designer of the twentieth century.

Shigure-tei 時雨亭. "Pavilion of the Autumn Rain," in the grounds of **Homyo-in Temple** in **Miidera** where **Ernest Fenollosa** and his friends used to stay.

Shimonoseki 下関市. City at the southwestern foot of Yamaguchi Prefecture. It overlooks the narrow Straits of Shimonoseki at the western end of the Inland Sea, separating the islands of Honshu and Kyushu.

Shingon Buddhism 真言宗. The second of the two largest sects of Esoteric Buddhism (*Mikkyo*), the other being **Tendai**. Founded by the monk Kukai at **Mount Koya** in 819.

Shinojima 篠島. A small island off the south coast of Aichi Prefecture, where **Owari Fief** used to exile criminals in Edo days.

shinryoku 新緑. "New green," a word for the fresh green foliage of early spring.

shin'yoju 針葉樹. "Needle-leaf" evergreen trees such as *hinoki* and *sugi* cedar.

shirakabe 白壁. "White plaster walls," mud walls surfaced with white plaster which stand on the roads in old towns, in front of temples, shrines and houses.

Shirakawa-go 白川郷. A famous village of high-ridged thatched houses in Gifu Prefecture.

Shirasu Masako 白洲正子(1910–1998). Art connoisseur, critic and writer, author of many books on Japanese history, art and travelogues, including *Hidden Hamlets*.

Shiroyone Rice Terraces 白米千枚田. Picturesque rice paddies on a slope overlooking the Sea of Japan on the north shore of the **Noto Peninsula**.

shishimai 獅子舞. "Lion dance," of which many striking examples are to be found in the **Tohoku** area.

Shizuki Castle 指月城. "Pointing-to-the-moon" Castle, the lord's castle of **Choshu Fief**, of which the ruins and moats survive in **Hagi City**.

Shizuki-yama 指月山. Mountain behind **Shizuki Castle** in **Hagi City**.

shochu 焼酎. Japanese-style vodka, made most often from potatoes, but also from rice, soba (buckwheat) or millet, ranging up to 45 proof.

Shodon 諸鈍. Village on the southeast shore of **Kakeroma** Island, **Amami**.

Shosoin Treasury 正倉院. A pair of wooden storehouses on the grounds of **Todaiji** Temple in Nara, built to house the treasures of **Emperor Shomu**, donated after his death by the Empress Komyo in 756.

Showa-mura 昭和村. Village to the north of **Minami-Aizu** town.

shugendo 修験道. Mystical practices performed by wandering ascetics in the mountains, a form of syncretic Shinto and *Mikkyo* (Esoteric) Buddhism.

Shukunegi 宿根木. A fishing village on the south coast of **Sado Island** in the Sea of Japan off the coast of Niigata City, Niigata Prefecture.

Sokuhi 即非如一 (1616–1671). Chinese monk of the **Obaku** sect of Zen, disciple of **Ingen**, known as one of the "Three Calligraphers of Obaku" 黄檗三筆.

somon 総門. Entry gate of a temple, usually smaller than the *sanmon* (main gate).

Song dynasty 宋朝. Chinese dynasty from 960–1279.

Soto Zen 曹洞宗. Largest of Japan's three major Zen sects, founded by Dogen in the thirteenth century, with head temples at Eiheiji in Fukui Prefecture and **Tsurumi** in Yokohama.

St. Joseph's College. A Catholic boy's school located in Yokohama on the Bluff next to the Foreigners Cemetery. Founded in 1888, it closed in 2000. Alex went here 1964–1966.

sugi スギ (杉). Cryptomeria cedar tree, used in construction and grown in forestry plantations across Japan.

Suo-no-kuni 周防国. The old feudal fief comprising the eastern half of what is now Yamaguchi Prefecture. In the early seventeenth century, it merged with **Naga-to-no-kuni** to become **Choshu Fief**.

Susa Hornfels 須佐ホルンフェルス. A rock formation in the Susa area north of **Hagi City** in Yamaguchi Prefecture, notable for its strong black and white stripes.

Suzu City 珠洲市. A city on the north shore of the **Noto Peninsula**.

Suzuki Satomi 鈴木里美. Freelance writer based in **Minami-Aizu**.

Tadaura Toyoji 只浦豊次. Owner of Misawaya 三澤屋 soba restaurant in **Ouchi-juku**, Fukushima Prefecture. Also owner of a huge stock of *kozai* wood from old houses.

tahoto 多宝塔. A type of pagoda typical of **Shingon** Buddhism, consisting of a square first story, a dome-shaped plaster middle section and a pyramidal tile roof.

Taira see **Heike**

Taira no Kiyomori 平清盛 (1118–1181). Warlord who dominated the late Heian era. After his death, the Taira (also called **Heike**) clan were defeated by **Minamoto Yoritomo** of the **Genji** clan, who established the Kamakura shogunate in 1185.

Taishin 諦心. "Heart of the Precepts," the name granted to **Ernest Fenollosa** on his initiation at **Homyo-in Temple** in **Miidera**.

Takagi, Jean-Marc 高木ジャン・マルク. French-Japanese resident of Amami, who with his wife, **Take Hisami**, has led the movement to try to save **Katoku** "Jurassic Beach."

Takagi Shinji 高木信治. Architect active in the **Wajima** area, who guided Alex and friends to sites on the **Noto Peninsula**.

Takarajima 宝島. "Treasure Islands," the name of a City of Tokyo committee focused on the islands belonging to Tokyo: the **Izu Archipelago** and **Ogasawara Islands**.

Takashima City 高島市. A city on the western shore of **Lake Biwa** in Shiga Prefecture.

Take Hisami 武久美. Wife of **Jean-Marc Takagi**, one of the leaders of the movement to save **Amami's Katoku** "Jurassic Beach."

Taketa City 竹田市. An old castle town in the Oita Prefecture, Kyushu.

tamenuri 溜塗り. A type of lacquer, semitransparent with a brownish maroon color verging on purple.

Tanabata 七夕. A festival, sometimes called the Star Festival held on the seventh day of the seventh month, to celebrate the reunion of the stars the Cowherd and the Weaving Girl on opposite sides of the universe, who can only meet once a year, on this day.

Tanaka Isson 田中一村. (1908–1977). A *Nihonga* (Japanese-style painter) painter in the primitivist mode, who spent his later years on the island of **Amami**. Virtually unknown in his lifetime, he achieved fame after his death, and there's now a museum dedicated to his works near Amami airport.

Tang dynasty 唐朝. Chinese dynasty from 618–907.

Tanso Shoemon 丹宗庄右衛門. Satsuma (present day Kagoshima) merchant in late Edo who was exiled to **Hachijojima** Island for illegal trading with the Qing Empire. In 1853 he introduced *shochu* distilled from potatoes to the **Izu Archipelago**.

Taru-mari タルマーリー. Name of bakery and brewery run by husband and wife **Watanabe Itaru and Mariko** in the town of Chizu, Tottori Prefecture.

Tashiro 田代. A village in the town of **Ugomachi** in Akita Prefecture, where **Butoh** dancer **Hijikata Tatsumi** and photographer **Hosoe Eiko** collaborated in taking the photographs that later became the book *Kama Itachi*.

Tendai 天台宗. One of the two major sects of *Mikkyo* (Esoteric Buddhism). Its history dates back to a temple founded in 538 on Mount Tiantai in China. When **Saicho** traveled to China, he studied at Mount Tiantai and brought back the temple's teachings to Japan, founding **Enryakuji Temple** on **Mount Hiei** in Kyoto in 806.

Tenjuin-seki 天樹院跡. The grounds of former Tenjuin Temple, containing **Mori clan** graves, in **Hagi City**, Yamaguchi Prefecture.

Tenkai 天海 (1536–1643). Long-lived crafty **Tendai** abbot who was advisor to **Tokugawa Ieyasu**, and the second and third shoguns after Ieyasu's death. Tenkai was instrumental in having Ieyasu deified as **Toshogu Daigongen**, and building the shogunal shrines (**Toshogu** shrines) in **Nikko**.

teramachi 寺町. "Temple neighborhood," the area in old towns set aside for temples and shrines.

Teratani Seiichiro 寺谷誠一郎. Mayor of **Chizu** town in southeastern Tottori Prefecture, retired in 2020. Founder of **Mitaki-en** restaurant in the hills outside of the town center, which is run by his wife **Teratani Setsuko**.

Teratani Setsuko 寺谷節子. Wife of former **Chizu** mayor **Teratani Seiichiro**, and *okami* (female proprietor) of **Mitaki-en** restaurant.

Tetsugaku-no-Michi 哲学の道. "Philosopher's Walk," a famous hillside walk in eastern Kyoto, lined by temples and shrines such as **Honen-in** Temple, the Tomb of Emperor Reizei, and Ginkakuji (Silver Pavilion).

Theory of Japanese Landscape ニッポン景観論. A book by Alex published in Japanese in 2014 on the subject of the degradation of the landscape caused by public works, over-signage and other issues, as well as offering some solutions for these problems.

Thirty-three Temples of Bando 坂東三十三観音. Pilgrimage route in the **Kanto** region of eastern Japan.

Thirty-three Temples of Western Japan see **Saikoku Sanjusansho**

Thirty-six Mystical Sites of En-no-Gyoja 役行者霊跡三十六札所. Pilgrimage route following sites associated with legendary ascetic and mystic En-no-gyoja (634–707).

Tobu Line 東武鉄道. Private railway line, starting at Asakusa in Tokyo and running north, with various branches.

tochi トチ (栃、橡). Japanese horse-chestnut tree.

Todaiji 東大寺. Hall of the Great Buddha in Nara, built by **Emperor Shomu** in 758. It was burned down by **Taira no Kiyomori** in 1181; rebuilt by Abbot Chogen in 1195; burned again in 1567; and rebuilt in 1709 (present structure). It's the largest wooden building in the world, and especially known for its massive wooden pillars.

Tohoku 東北. Northern Japan, comprising six prefectures north of Tokyo, from Fukushima up to Aomori.

Tojinbo 東尋坊. Famous viewing spot of cliffs and rocks along the Sea of Japan in Sakai City, Fukui Prefecture.

Tokoji Temple 東光寺. Temple in **Hagi City**, Yamaguchi Prefecture, belonging to the **Obaku** Zen sect. It contains ancestral graves of the **Mori clan**, lords of **Choshu Fief**.

Tokugawa Iemitsu 徳川家光 (1604–1651, reigned 1623–1651). Third shogun of the Edo period.

Tokugawa Ietsuna 徳川家綱 (1641–1680, reigned 1651–1680). Fourth shogun of the Edo period.

Tokugawa Ieyasu 徳川家康 (1543–1616, shogun after 1603). Founder and first shogun of the Edo period. After his death, he was deified as **Toshogu Daigongen** and buried at **Toshogu Shrine** in **Nikko**.

Tomonoura 鞆の浦. An old harbor on the Inland Sea in Hiroshima Prefecture, known for a precedent-making lawsuit in which government plans to landfill the harbor were denied by the courts in 2009.

Toshima 利島. From the mainland coast, the second of the **Seven Islands of the Izu Archipelago**.

Toshogu Daigongen 東照宮大権現. Deified posthumous title of **Tokugawa Ieyasu**.

Toshogu Shrine 東照宮. The shrine in **Nikko** where **Tokugawa Ieyasu** is buried. Also the name of several dozen other shrines dedicated to Ieyasu located across Japan.

Toshogu-zukuri 東照宮造り. The style of colorful super-decorated shrine found at **Toshogu Shrine** in Nikko and other **Toshogu** shrines.

Tottori Sand Dunes 鳥取砂丘. Extensive sand dunes on the northeast shore of Tottori Prefecture.

Tour of Imperial Tombs 天皇陵巡り. Pilgrimage route of 124 imperial tombs.

Toyotomi Hideyoshi 豊臣秀吉 (1537–1598). Second of the three great warlords of the late sixteenth century. He succeeded **Oda Nobunaga**, who had unified Japan after a century of domestic warfare, and consolidated central rule. He was followed by **Tokugawa Ieyasu** who founded the Edo shogunate.

True Record of Hachijo 八丈実記. A book written by **Kondo Tomizo** who was exiled to **Hachijojima** Island in 1826.

Tsubouchi Shoyo 坪内逍遥 (1859–1935). Prominent novelist, critic and playwright, a disciple of **Ernest Fenollosa**, along with **Okakura Tenshin**.

tsuga ツガ (栂). A tree related to pine, Japanese hemlock.

Tsurumi 鶴見. Northeastern ward of Yokohama (and also the name of its train station), site of Sojiji Temple, head temple of the **Soto Zen** sect.

Ugomachi 羽後町. A township in southern Akita Prefecture, within which is the village of **Tashiro**, where **Hijikata Tatsumi** and **Hosoe Eiko** staged the photographs for the book *Kama Itachi*.

uni ウニ (雲丹). Sea urchin.

ura 裏. "The back" or "behind." Used for places or ideas which are hidden and esoteric. Contrasts with *omote* "the front," things that are well-known or easily accessible.

Ura-Nihon 裏日本. "The back of Japan," used to refer to the Sea of Japan coast.

Ushi-to 牛塔. "Cow Monument," a stone memorial dedicated to a cow who labored in the rebuilding of **Sekidera** Temple in **Otsu City** in the early eleventh century. Thought to have been built in the thirteenth century.

Ushi ni hikarete Zenkoji mairi 「牛に引かれて善光寺参り」. An old saying: "Drawn by a cow to worship at Zenkoji Temple."

Ushio-gu 牛尾宮. One of the pair of buildings, along with **Sannomiya**, at the **Oku-no-Miya** inner sanctuary of **Hiyoshi Taisha** Shrine.

wabi and *sabi* 詫びと寂び. Rustic simplicity (*wabi*) and the wear of age (*sabi*)—terms used in Japanese aesthetics.

Wajima City 輪島市. City on the north shore of the **Noto Peninsula**, known for its lacquer production.

Wajima lacquer 輪島塗. Famed lacquerware produced in **Wajima City**.

Wakuden 和久傳. One of the top **kaiseki** restaurants of Kyoto.

Watanabe Itaru and Mariko 渡邉格、麻里子. Proprietors of the bakery and brewery **Taru-Mari** in **Chizu** town, Tottori Prefecture.

wayo 和洋. "Japanese style," a term used in traditional arts, in distinction to *karayo* 唐洋 "Chinese style." Wayo tends to be soft, feminine, delicate, refined, and focused on the "little things" of nature, like moss and grasses.

Woods, James Haughton (1864–1935). Harvard professor who translated Sanskrit and Pali texts into English; he arranged for the first classes in Japanese culture ever taught at Harvard. His tomb is at **Homyo-in Temple** in **Miidera**.

Yakushima Island 屋久島. A southern island located between **Amami** and Okinawa, known for its primeval jungles with ancient *sugi* cedar trees.

Yamada Arisa 山田アリサ. Manager of small factory making salt distilled using *hingya* (volcanic ground steam) on **Aogashima** Island.

Yamaguchi City 山口市. Capital of Yamaguchi Prefecture. Base of the **Ouchi clan** from the fourteenth to sixteenth century, it was incorporated into **Choshu Fief** in 1591. In 1863 the capital of the fief was moved here from **Hagi City** where it remained until the disestablishment of the fief with the **Meiji Restoration** (1868).

Yamato-e 大和絵. "Japanese images," used in contrast to Chinese-style ink painting. Yamato-e is rich in color, depicts round Japanese hills instead of high Chinese peaks, with an abundance of grasses and wildflowers.

Yamazaki Takayuki 山崎貴之. Young employee of the company **One Story**, who sponsors the **Dining Out** events. Yamazaki arranged for the tour in **Minami-Aizu** which Alex guided.

Yanagida Kunio 柳田国男 (1875–1962). Renowned ethnologist who researched local legends around Japan. Known for his *Tales of Tono* 遠野物語 and *Record of the Return to Aogashima*.

Yazu 八頭町. A town in the interior of southeastern Tottori Prefecture, location of **Seitokuji Temple**.

Yokosuka City 横須賀市. A city on the eastern shore of the **Miura Peninsula**, home of a large US naval base, where Alex's father was stationed in the 1960s.

Yoshimura Norio 吉村徳男. Owner of Komeya soba restaurant (そば処こめや) in the historic inn town of **Ouchi-juku**, Fukushima Prefecture. He left his job at the local town office to become a professional roof thatcher.

Yuan dynasty 元朝. Chinese dynasty from 1271–1368.

Yuhi-no-oka 夕日の丘. "Sunset Hill," viewing spot on **Kakeroma** Island, south of **Amami** Island, overlooking the **Oshima Strait**.

Zecha, Adrian (1933–). Legendary hotel developer, who created the Aman Resorts in Bali and Thailand, which later expanded worldwide. After selling Aman in the 2013, Zecha founded Azerai in Laos (2017) and Azumi in Japan (2021).

Zuiryuji 瑞龍寺. A grand **Soto Zen** temple in Takaoka City, Toyama Prefecture. Founded by Maeda Toshinaga, first lord of **Kaga Fief** in 1614.

Zushi City 逗子市. A city on the western shore of the **Miura Peninsula**, between Kamakura and **Hayama**.